ideas

ideas

+spaces
+espacios
+espaces
+räume

AUTHORS
Fernando de Haro & Omar Fuentes

EDITORIAL DESIGN & PRODUCTION

EDITORES

PROJECT MANAGERS
Valeria Degregorio Vega
Tzacil Cervantes Ortega

COORDINATION
Susana Madrigal Gutiérrez

COPYWRITER
Roxana Villalobos

ENGLISH TRANSLATION
Louis Loizides

FRENCH TRANSLATION
Architextos: Translation Services and Language Solutions

GERMAN TRANSLATION
Heike Ruttkowski

Ideas
+spaces · +espacios · +espaces · +räume

© 2010, Fernando de Haro & Omar Fuentes

AM Editores S.A. de C.V.
Paseo de Tamarindos 400 B, suite 102, Col. Bosques de las Lomas,
C.P. 05120, México, D.F. Tels. 52(55) 5258 0279, Fax. 52(55) 5258 0556.
E-mail: ame@ameditores.com   www.ameditores.com

ISBN 13: 978-607-437-035-5

Printed in China.

14

INDEX · INDICE

introduction introducción

UNDERSTANDING THE CHARACTERISTICS OF A SPACE and how they can be used is essential for defining a project and its esthetic qualities. Just as important is the role of light and color in this definition, but there is also style, which is very closely linked to personal preferences and the trends of the times.

The more attention we pay to the specific determining factors, functions and needs of a place, as well as individual taste, the better and more unique the results and decorative impact will be.

ENTENDER LAS CARACTERÍSTICAS DEL ESPACIO y sus usos ayuda a definir correctamente el proyecto y su estética. Las soluciones de diseño, así como el empleo del color y la luz son herramientas necesarias para concretar dicha definición. Pero además existen estilos, que están íntimamente relacionados con los gustos personales, y tendencias, que responden a modas.

Cuanto más se consideren las condicionantes, funciones y necesidades particulares del lugar y las preferencias individuales, tanto mejores resultados y pautas decorativas con carácter propio se alcanzarán.

introduction   einleitung

POUR DÉFINIR CORRECTEMENT UN PROJET DÉCORATIF et l'esthétique qui va avec, il est utile de comprendre les caractéristiques de l'espace à décorer et l'utilisation qui l'on va en faire. Le type de design et l'usage que l'on va faire de la couleur et de la lumière sont des outils nécessaires pour mener à bien une telle entreprise. Mais il faut aussi prendre en compte les différents styles existants, ce qui relève des goûts de chacun, ainsi que les tendances actuelles en rapport avec les modes.

Plus on réfléchit sur les fonctions, les nécessités et les conditions propres à l'espace à décorer, plus on prend

EINE ANALYSE DER EIGENSCHAFTEN EINES RAUMES und dessen Gebrauch hilft in Bezug auf die korrekte Definition des Projektes und dessen Ästhetik. Die Designlösungen, sowie der Gebrauch von Farbe und Licht sind Werkzeuge, die zur Konkretisierung dieser Definiton erforderlich sind. Ausserdem gibt es Stilrichtungen, die sich strikt nach den persönlichen Vorlieben richten, sowie auch nach Trends, die gerade modern sind.

Je mehr Bedingungen, Funktionen, besondere Erfordernisse des Ortes und individuelle Vorlieben

Design, color and light offer many options for creating a space but it is crucial to think about how they interact together and can become transformed in a given place. For instance, the visual dimension can be set by using colors and textures, and then modified by the effect of the lighting. At the same time, light could act one way or another depending on the color it comes into contact with and on the tone of light used. The use of daylight requires taking into account its gradual transformations over the course of the day.

These spatial interrelations will generate the ambience and define the overall look of a place, as well as the impact on the senses. Furthermore, they afford meaning for the people who live there; in other words, they generate stimuli and ultimately the experience offered by the space.

Sin embargo, aunque bien las soluciones de diseño, color y luz son medios para moldear el espacio, es imprescindible meditar la manera en la que estos elementos interactúan entre sí en un sitio determinado y analizar cómo se transforman. Por ejemplo, la dimensión visual se concreta con el manejo del color y las texturas, pero puede ser modificada por los efectos de la iluminación o, en sentido contrario, la luz puede actuar de una u otra forma según sea el color con el que haga contacto y dependiendo del tono de la luminaria que se use (incluso, cuando interviene la luz natural es también importante tomar en cuenta sus mutaciones a diversas horas del día).

Todas estas interrelaciones espaciales son las que van generando un ambiente y precisan su estética, pero también funcionan para provocar la respuesta de los sentidos y hacer que el espacio adquiera significado para quien lo habite; es decir,

en compte les préférences personnelles de chacun et plus on sera à même d'obtenir un résultat satisfaisant avec des choix décoratifs originaux.

Cependant, même si les solutions concernant le design, la couleur et la lumière constituent des moyens de transformer l'espace selon ses goûts, il est indispensable de réfléchir à l'interaction de tous ses éléments dans un endroit précis et d'analyser leurs rôles ensemble. Par exemple, la couleur et les textures sont essentielles pour créer une dimension visuelle esthétique qui peut parfois être modifiée par la lumière. En revanche, cette lumière peut être l'élément principal pour d'autres espaces visuels car les couleurs éclairées réagissent toutes de multiples façons et tout dépend de la teinte choisie pour l'éclairage (il ne faut pas non plus oublier le rôle joué par la lumière naturelle et penser à ses effets tout au long de la journée).

mit einbezogen werden, desto vorteilhafter sind die Ergebnisse und dekorativen Richtlinien mit eigenem Charakter, die erzielt werden.

Obwohl Designlösungen, Farbe und Licht dazu dienen, den Raum zu formen, ist es dennoch unabdingbar darauf einzuwirken, wie diese Elemente untereinander in einem bestimmten Raum zusammenwirken; ferner sollte ihre Umsetzung analysiert werden. So wird zum Beispiel die visuelle Dimension durch die Handhabung von Farbe und Texturen konkretisiert, dies kann aber durch die Beleuchtungseffekte verändert werden; oder das Licht kann -ganz im Gegensatz dazu- auf die eine oder andere Weise wirken, je nachdem, welche Farbe Verwendung findet und in Abhängigkeit vom Farbton der eingesetzten Beleuchtung (sogar wenn natürliches Licht zur Anwendung kommt ist es wichtig, dessen Veränderung zu unterschiedlichen Tageszeiten in Betracht zu ziehen).

Choosing the design, color and lighting for a home is clearly a different prospect from doing so for a work space or commercial premises. Decorations in a store or leisure center need to be more prominent and intense than in a home or office, where a more relaxed setting is the order of the day.

Needless to say, the most interesting spaces are the ones that evoke a series of sensations as people pass through them. Creating such an effect does not necessarily involve enlisting an endless array of decorative devices; it simply means choosing the most suitable and effective options.

There is a huge range of textures, materials, shapes, colors and lights to choose from in order to create original settings with a personal touch. The key is to be aware of the different variables that come into play when defining an area and paying attention to comfort, practicality and look. The expressional preferences of the people who will occupy the space in question, along with their interests and concept of comfort, are all vital factors that designers need to take into account to ensure a successful solution.

son generadoras de estímulos y, por lo tanto, de experiencias espaciales.

Desde luego, es obvio que no es lo mismo especificar el diseño, el color o la iluminación para una vivienda que para un espacio de trabajo o para áreas comerciales. Las decoraciones comerciales tanto como las de los espacios destinados al entretenimiento admiten estímulos más intensos y agresivos que las de una casa u oficina, en las que se prefieren atmósferas más relajadas.

Está por demás decir que los espacios más interesantes son aquéllos que al recorrerlos van engendrando sensaciones que se suceden unas a otras, y que para alcanzar este objetivo no es necesario recurrir a un festín de efectos decorativos, sino simplemente abocarse a elegir aquéllos que sean más adecuados y efectivos.

Hay una gran paleta de texturas, materiales, formas, colores y luces para elegir y crear ambientes propios y originales, solamente hay que estar atento a las distintas variables que conforman el universo de cada área y cuidar su comodidad, funcionalidad y estética. Es innegable que la expresión de las personas que van a ocupar esos ambientes, sus intereses y el concepto que tienen de confort son los aspectos fundamentales a los que el diseñador tiene que dar respuestas contundentes.

Les interrelations existantes entre tous ces éléments créent des atmosphères et une esthétique particulières. Elles stimulent également les sensations de celui ou celle qui réside dans cet espace, lui permettant de le comprendre. En d'autres mots, tous ces éléments provoquent diverses sensations et, en conséquence, différentes impressions par rapport à cet espace.

Concevoir le design, la couleur et l'éclairage d'un lieu de vie est évidemment différent lorsqu'il s'agit d'un espace de travail ou d'un endroit destiné à une activité commerciale. Les décorations pour un commerce _c'est aussi le cas pour les espaces de loisir_ admettent des stimulants plus intenses et plus vifs que dans une maison ou un bureau où l'on cherchera à créer une atmosphère plus tranquille.

Il va sans dire que les espaces les plus intéressants sont ceux où les sensations que l'on ressent en les parcourant sont multiples et variées. Pour parvenir à concevoir de tels lieux, il n'est pas nécessaire d'avoir recours à une pléthore d'effets décoratifs. Mieux vaut plutôt opter pour les plus indiqués et les plus utiles parmi eux.

La gamme des textures, des matériaux, des formes, des couleurs et des lumières est très large lorsque l'on désire créer des atmosphères personnelles et originales. Il est toutefois nécessaire de prendre en compte les particularités propres à l'espace en question et de soigner ses aspects pratique, fonctionnel et esthétique. De plus, le designer doit indéniablement apporter des réponses convaincantes aux attentes fondamentales des personnes qui vont occuper l'espace et à la conception qu'elles se font du confort.

All diese Wechselspiele im Raum verfeinern die Ästhetik und führen zu einer bestimmten Atmosphäre. Sie regen aber auch die Sinne an und verleihen dem Raum eine Bedeutung für seine Bewohner, das heisst, es werden Reize geschaffen und somit auch räumliche Erfahrungen.

Es ist natürlich nicht dasselbe, das Design, die Farbe und die Beleuchtung für ein Wohnhaus, einen Arbeitsbereich oder ein Einkaufszentrun zu bestimmen. Die Dekoration in Einkaufzentren und Bereichen, die der Unterhaltung gewidmet sind, erlauben viel intensivere und aggresivere Reize als in einem Haus oder einem Büro, in denen eine entspanntere Atmosphäre vorgezogen wird.

Es versteht sich von selbst, dass die interessantesten Orte diejenigen sind, die nacheinander Empfindungen hervorrufen; dabei sollte dieses Ziel nicht durch eine Vielzahl an dekorativen Effekten erreicht werden, sondern durch die Wahl derjenigen Details, die am geeignetsten und effektivsten sind.

Es ist eine grosse Auswahl an Texturen, Materialien, Formen, Farben und Lichtern vorhanden, mit denen bestimmte, originelle Atmosphären geschaffen werden können. Dabei ist nur auf die verschiedenen Variablen zu achten, die das Universum eines jeden Bereiches ausmachen, wobei auch die Bequemlichkeit, Funktionalität und Ästhetik nicht zu vernachlässigen sind. Es steht ausser Frage, dass der Ausdruck der Personen, die diese Atmophären bewohnen werden, ihre Interessen und das Konzept, das sie von Komfort haben, die grundlegenden Aspekte sind, auf die ein Designer überzeugende Antworten finden muss.

color
couleur
farbe

COLOR plays a decisive role in the interior decor of modern-day offices, especially when it comes to arousing different sensations. For example, a dynamic and vibrant ambience can be achieved using high-saturation primary and secondary colors; but their impact will need to be balanced in order to project harmony and blend in with the white decoration and/or natural wood hues.

EL COLOR es un elemento determinante en el interiorismo de las oficinas contemporáneas y se le puede utilizar para evocar sensaciones. Por ejemplo, si se desea proyectar un sitio dinámico y vibrante, los colores primarios y secundarios, en su nivel de saturación más elevado, son los idóneos; pero será necesario equilibrar su energía, para también expresar ecuanimidad, añadiendo a la decoración blanco y/o las tonalidades de la madera natural.

LA COULEUR est un élément déterminant pour la décoration intérieure d'espaces professionnels modernes et il est possible de l'utiliser pour donner une atmosphère particulière à un endroit. Par exemple, si l'on souhaite dynamiser l'espace, en faire un lieu plein d'énergie, les couleurs primaires et secondaires très vives sont on ne peut plus indiquées. Il conviendra toutefois d'équilibrer l'énergie dégagée afin d'uniformiser l'endroit en ajoutant du blanc à la décoration ou en mettant en relief les teintes du bois naturel (on peut également faire les deux).

offices
oficinas
bureaux
büros

FARBE ist ein bestimmendes Element im Innendesign von modernen Büros und kann dazu verwendet werden, bestimmte Eindrücke zu erwecken. Soll zum Beispiel ein dynamischer und schwungvoller Ort geschaffen werden, sind Pirmär- und Sekundärfarben mit höchster Sättigung am geeignetsten. Dabei sollte aber in Bezug auf die Energie ein Gleichgewicht geschaffen werden, um auch eine Gleichmässigkeit zum Ausdruck zu bringen, wobei weisse Farbe und/oder natürliche Holztöne Verwendung finden.

If the purpose and nature of the different items and materials, respectively, of an office are left undisguised, a feeling of industriousness will be generated, as the decorative ambience is reminiscent of a factory. However, it is not a bad idea to use color to add a touch of warmth and movement. Brownish-red and pale green are very much in synch with the factory look and look great if combined with some kind of graphic expression.

Cuando las instalaciones y los materiales de una oficina son expuestos tal cual son sin ocultar su función, en el caso de las primeras, y su naturaleza, en el de los segundos, se consigue dar la impresión de productividad, pues el ambiente decorativo recuerda al de las fábricas. Conviene, sin embargo, agregar un toque de calidez y movimiento al espacio valiéndose del color. El verde y el rojo, en sus matices quemados, siguen la línea decorativa fabril y se ven excepcionales si se les agrega algún grafismo.

On peut donner à des bureaux une ambiance industrieuse si l'on ne cache pas leur infrastructure et si les matériaux qui entrent dans leur construction sont utilisés à l'état brut. La décoration fera alors penser aux locaux des usines. Il convient cependant d'ajouter une touche de chaleur et de mouvement avec certaines couleurs. Le vert et le rouge, dans des tons foncés, sont tout indiqués pour le style industriel. Si l'on y ajoute des éléments graphiques, leur présence n'en sera que plus remarquable.

Wenn die Einrichtungen und Materialien eines Büros so wie sie sind dargestellt werden, ohne ihre Funktion zu verbergen, wird der Eindruck von Produktivität erweckt, denn die dekorative Atmosphäre erinnert an die einer Fabrik. Es ist dennoch angebracht, dem Raum einen Touch Wärme und Bewegung hinzuzufügen, wobei Farbe zum Einsatz kommt. Grün und Rot in ihren gebrannten Nuancen, passen dekorativ in die Fabrikatmosphäre und sehen besonders attraktiv aus, wenn ein graphisches Detail hinzugefügt wird.

IT'S LUNCH TIME!

TOMARSE MUY EN SERIO LOS SUEÑ

TE, HAY QUE TOMARSE MUY EN SERIO LOS SUEÑ

COMEDOR

Pure white is associated with cleanliness and order, both of which can be accentuated through the use of pure lines, right angles, smooth surfaces, transparencies and just a touch of color.

Al blanco puro se le relaciona con la limpieza y el orden, características que se acrecientan si también juegan en la composición decorativa líneas puras, ángulos rectos, planos lisos, transparencias y se introduce un toque de color.

Le blanc pur donne une impression de propreté et d'ordre, caractéristiques que l'on peut renforcer si des lignes pures, des angles droits, des surfaces lisses et des éléments transparents jouent un rôle dans l'ensemble de la décoration et si l'on y ajoute une touche de couleur.

Die Farbe weiss wird mit Reinheit und Ordnung in Verbindung gebracht, wobei es sich um Eigenschaften handelt, die noch verstärkt werden, wenn die Dekoration klare Linien, rechte Winkel, Transparenz und nur einen Touch Farbe aufweist.

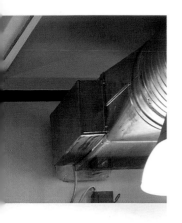

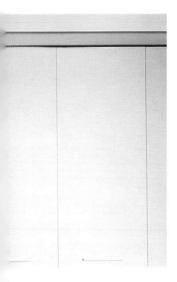

The interplay of highly polished red and white surfaces with silver toned objects and materials and lighting guided to create reflection offers an interesting range of esthetic options and brings out unexpected qualities of color and texture.

Si en un mismo espacio interactúan superficies blancas y rojas muy pulidas, elementos y materiales en tonalidades plata y una iluminación orientada a producir reflejos, las posibilidades estéticas de la atmósfera se potencian y se revelan cualidades insospechadas del color y la textura.

Si, dans un même espace, on associe des surfaces polies blanches et rouges avec des éléments et des matériaux couleur argent et un éclairage orienté afin de produire des reflets, les possibilités esthétiques de l'atmosphère ainsi créée sont plus vastes et les qualités de la couleur et de la texture produisent alors des effets inespérés.

Wenn in einem Raum hochpolierte, weisse und rote Oberflächen vorhanden sind, sowie Elemente und Materialien in Silberfarben und eine Beleuchtung, die Reflexe hervorruft, so sind den ästhetischen Möglichkeiten keine Grenzen gesetzt und es entstehen ungeahnte Qualitäten in Bezug auf Farbe und Textur.

A skillful combination of brown, terra cotta and orange tones will generate a lively working environment.

A través de la combinación de cafés, terracotas y naranjas se asegura un contexto laboral dinámico.

L'association des couleurs marron, terre-cuite et orange dans des tons variés dynamise à coup sûr l'espace professionnel.

Durch eine Kombination von Braun, Terrakotta und Orange wird ein dynamischer Arbeitskontext sichergestellt.

In decorative terms, a place is considered chromatically neutral if its range is derived from black, white or gray; but a similar outcome is also achieved through the use of beige and brown, or even the natural tones of certain materials. One good option is to break the monotony by including an architectural or decorative element in a highly saturated color. Saturated colors look particularly good when used on transparent and translucent materials (glass or plastic) and are placed in front of a light source.

En términos decorativos un lugar es considerado cromáticamente neutro cuando su gama se deriva del negro, blanco o gris, pero también los beiges y cafés o el dominio del color natural de los materiales hacen pensar en sitios neutrales. Una opción decorativa es romper la monotonía introduciendo algún elemento arquitectónico o decorativo en un color muy saturado. Los saturados son tonos que lucen particularmente atractivos si se les usa sobre materiales transparentes y translúcidos (vítreos o plásticos) y se les coloca frente a una fuente de la fuente de luz.

En décoration, on considère qu'un lieu est chromatiquement neutre lorsque les couleurs que l'on y relève dérivent du noir, du blanc ou du gris. Mais les beiges ou les marrons, ainsi que les couleurs naturelles des matériaux utilisés à l'état brut, font aussi penser à des endroits de couleur neutre. Il est possible de rompre cette uniformité chromatique en y insérant un élément architectural ou décoratif de couleur très vive. Les teintes vives sont particulièrement esthétiques si on les place sur des matériaux transparents ou translucides (verre ou plastique) et face à une source de lumière.

Im dekorativen Sinne ist ein Ort chromatisch neutral, wenn sich die Farbtöne von den Farben schwarz, weiss und grau ableiten. Aber auch beige und braun oder vorwiegend natürliche Töne der Materialien erwecken den Eindruck eines neutralen Ortes. Eine dekorative Möglichkeit ist es, die Monotonie durch ein architektonisches oder dekoratives Element zu durchbrechen, das einen sehr gesättigten Farbton aufweist. Die gesättigten Farbtöne sehen besonders attratkiv aus, wenn sie auf transparenten und durchscheinenden Materialien (Glas oder Plastik) verwendet werden, die sich vor einer Lichtquelle befinden.

Designed to work. Built to last.

The frequency with which the same color features in a given space – such as two green objects, two orange objects – can give a place a very appealing chromatic and visual rhythm.

La frecuencia con la que aparece un mismo color en el espacio, por ejemplo dos objetos verdes, dos elementos naranjas… puede dar lugar a un ritmo cromático y a una cadencia visual muy atractiva.

Lorsqu'une même couleur est utilisée à plusieurs reprises dans l'espace (avec, par exemple, deux objets verts, deux accessoires oranges …), on peut créer un certain rythme chromatique, une cadence visuelle très attrayante.

Die Häufigkeit, mit der dieselbe Farbe in einem Raum zu sehen ist, zum Beispiel zwei grüne Objekte, zwei orange Objekte, führt zu einem chromatischen Rhythmus und zu einem sehr attraktiven, visuellen Takt.

restaurants
restaurantes

THE COLOR PALETTE of a restaurant needs to be subtle, as colors will affect the mood and preferences of diners. For instance, some people choose certain drinks more for their color than for their flavor. Color schemes based on red, yellow and orange stimulate people and make them stay longer; but given that these colors also enhance the sensation of proximity they are more suitable for spacious settings.

LA PALETA CROMÁTICA de un restaurante es delicada, pues los colores influyen en el estado de ánimo y preferencias de las personas; por ejemplo, hay bebidas que son más solicitadas por su color que por su sabor. Aquellas composiciones con base en el rojo, amarillo y anaranjado estimulan a la gente para que permanezca más tiempo en un lugar; no obstante, dado que son colores que incrementan el efecto de cercanía, se recomiendan para espacios amplios.

LA PALETTE CHROMATIQUE d'un restaurant est délicate à constituer car les couleurs jouent un rôle important sur l'humeur et les choix des clients. On sait, par exemple, que certaines boissons sont choisies non pour leur goût mais pour leur teinte. Une décoration basée sur le rouge, le jaune et l'orange incite les personnes présentes à rester plus longtemps. Mais comme ces couleurs accentuent l'effet de proximité, elles sont recommandées pour des espaces plutôt vastes.

DIE CHROMATISCHE PALETTE eines Restaurants ist wichtig, denn die Farben beeinflussen den Gemütszustand und die Vorlieben der Personen. Es gibt zum Beispiel Getränke, die mehr aufgrund ihrer Farbe als aufgrund ihres Geschmacks beliebt sind. Kombinationen in rot, gelb und orange stimulieren die Gäste zum Verbleib am Ort. Dennoch ist zu berücksichtigen, dass diese Farben den Effekt von Nähe verstärken, sie sind daher nur in grossen Räumen empfehlenswert.

One good way to create a pervasive, stylish and cozy ambience is to give white and brown an equally dominant role in a given space, and then break this with a vibrant orange in a prominent location along with a few smaller details in yellow and orange.

Una alternativa para evocar un ambiente tenaz, elegante y a la vez acogedor es dejar al blanco y al café dominar equilibradamente el espacio, para luego romper con un naranja enérgico en una zona focalizada e incluir pequeños detalles en amarillo y naranja.

Afin de faire d'un endroit un lieu élégant, accueillant et avec du caractère, il est possible d'opter pour une dominante chromatique équilibrée à base de blanc et de marron. Mais il faut ensuite rompre cette uniformité avec un orange vif dans une zone précise et ajouter quelques petits détails jaunes et orange.

Eine Alternative für eine beharrliche, elegante und gleichzeitig gemütliche Atmosphäre bieten die Farben weiss und braun, die ausgeglichen verwendet werden sollten. Dann kann mit einem energischen Orange ein bestimmter Bereich abgehoben werden und zusätzlich werden kleine Details in gelb und orange gehalten.

A vibrant tone on different visual planes will liven up the decor. The more the visual angle opens up, the more the color's accent and rhythm will come to life.

Intervenir diferentes planos espaciales con un matiz potente le da un aspecto vivaz a la decoración y, a medida que el ángulo visual se abra, se irá captando la cadencia y el acento del color.

Une décoration vivante, c'est par exemple faire jouer différentes surfaces dans l'espace avec une teinte très vive. Plus notre regard s'amplifie et plus nous sommes à même d'apprécier le rythme et les particularités de la couleur utilisée.

Werden verschiedene räumliche Ebenen mit einem kräftigen Farbton versehen, so verleiht dies der Dekoration einen lebendigen Eindruck. Der visuelle Winkel wird geöffnet und der Rhythmus und der Akzent, der mit Farbe gesetzt wurde, werden deutlich.

One failsafe decorative option is to leave the strongest color for the deepest architectural element, as this will define the place's finishing touches and focal point. It will also highlight the shape of the different objects, such as bottles, sculptures, collections, ornaments and other things.

Una opción decorativa infalible es dejar el color más intenso para el elemento arquitectónico de mayor profundidad, con ello se puntualiza que es el remate y punto focal del lugar. Esta posibilidad permite, además, destacar las formas de los objetos, ya sean botellas, esculturas, colecciones, adornos, entre otros.

Une solution décorative infaillible consiste à utiliser une couleur particulière pour l'élément architectural le plus éloigné. Ce dernier devient alors l'élément-clé de l'endroit, celui qui attire notre regard. Cette solution permet également de mettre en relief les formes de certains objets comme, par exemple, des bouteilles, des sculptures, des collections d'objets ou des éléments décoratifs.

Eine dekorative Alternative, die immer gern verwendet wird, ist es, das tiefste architektonische Element mit einer intensiven Farbe zu versehen. So kann hervorgehoben werden, dass es sich um den zentralen Punkt des Ortes handelt. Diese Möglichkeit erlaubt es ferner, die Formen von Objekten zu betonen, gleichgültig ob es sich dabei um Flaschen, Skulpturen, Sammlungen, Dekor oder sonstiges handelt.

SHOPPING MALLS are semi-public places visited by many people. This means that their interior design needs to take many different tastes into account, have its own personality but, at the same time, not clash with the look of the stores they house. One way to satisfy these requirements is to use a neutral base on most of the surfaces coupled with a stronger color on some select architectural elements near the elevators, toilets, telephones, information desks and on the signs.

LOS CENTROS COMERCIALES son lugares semi-públicos y concurridos cuyo diseño interior debe responder con efectividad a muchos gustos, gozar de personalidad y no competir con el de los comercios que albergan. Usar como base un colorido neutro en la mayor parte de las superficies y un tono recio en algunos elementos arquitectónicos de las zonas de elevadores, baños, teléfonos, información y en la señalización, es un recurso que resuelve muchas de las demandas mencionadas.

LES CENTRES COMMERCIAUX sont des endroits semi-publics et très fréquentés. Leur design intérieur doit essayer de répondre aux attentes les plus diverses. Ce sont en général des designs très personnalisés mais qui n'étouffent pas ceux choisis par les commerces qu'on y trouve. Pour y parvenir, on utilise d'ordinaire des couleurs neutres pour la plupart des surfaces et des teintes très vives pour quelques éléments architecturaux comme les panneaux de signalisation et les endroits où l'on trouve les ascenseurs, les W-C, les téléphones et des renseignements.

EINKAUFSZENTREN sind öffentliche und sehr frequentierte Orte, deren Innendesign die Geschmäcker vieler Menschen befriedigen muss und Persönlichkeit zeigen sollte. Dabei darf aber nicht mit den Geschäften konkurriert werden, die darin beherbert sind. Die Grundlage sollte eine neutrale Farbpalette für die meisten Oberflächen bilden, sowie ein auffälliger Farbton an einigen architektonischen Elementen, wie Aufzüge, Toiletten, Telefone, Information und Ausschilderung. Diese Alternative befriedigt viele der vorgenannten Erfordernisse.

miscellaneous spaces
espacios diversos
lieux divers
verschiedene bereiche

A single vibrant tone can frame the façade's architectural finery and grab the attention of passers-by.

Un solo tono vibrante basta para enmarcar los detalles de la arquitectura de una fachada y llamar la atención de los transeúntes.

Une seule teinte vive suffit pour souligner les détails architecturaux d'une façade et attirer le regard des passants.

Ein einziger leuchtender Farbton ist ausreichend, um Details der Architektur einer Fassade einzurahmen und die Aufmerksamkeit der Passanten auf sich zu ziehen.

movie theaters cines cinémas kinos

One characteristic of movie theater complexes is the sharp contrast between the screening rooms and the other areas, such as the façade-marquee, corridors, antechambers, store and the soda fountain. The darkness of the former is a far cry from the bright lights and decor of the latter, whose colors are considered by psychologists to make people happy. Some experts even claim that orange allows people to release negative emotions and feel more at home.

En los complejos de cine se vive un marcado contraste entre las zonas de exhibición de las películas –las salas– y el resto de las áreas –fachada-marquesina, corredores, ante-salas, tienda, fuente de sodas…–. La oscura atmósfera de las primeras invita a crear un marcado contraste con la decoración de las segundas, incluyendo colores luminosos que, además, son considerados por los especialistas en psicología del color como alegres. Incluso, algunos de ellos afirman que la luminosidad del naranja propicia que la gente libere emociones negativas y se sienta acogida.

Pour les multiplex et autres cinémas, on créé un contraste très marqué entre les lieux où l'on assiste à la projection des films (les salles) et les autres espaces (la façade, l'entrée principale, les couloirs, le hall, les petits magasins comme la fontaine de sodas …). L'obscurité des salles incite en effet à l'utilisation de couleurs lumineuses pour la décoration des autres endroits. Ces couleurs vives sont associées par les psychologues à la joie, à la gaité. Certains d'entre eux affirment même que la couleur orange incite les gens à évacuer leurs émotions négatives et à se sentir plus à l'aise dans ces endroits.

In Kinos besteht ein krasser Gegensatz zwischen den Bereichen, an denen Filme gesehen werden – den Vorführräumen – und den übrigen Bereichen, wie Fassade, Dach, Gänge, Vorräume, Geschäfte und Getränkeverkauf. Die dunkle Atmosphäre ersterer unterscheidet sich merklich von der Dekoration letzterer, wobei auch leuchtende Farben Verwendung finden, die durch Spezialisten im Bereich der Psychologie als fröhlich eingestuft werden. Einige von ihnen bestätigen, dass leuchtendes Orange dazu führt, dass Menschen negative Gefühle vergessen und sich wohl fühlen.

It is necessary to bear in mind the importance in interior decoration of the natural colors of materials because of their ability to change the perception of space in a given area. Metals like stainless steel, aluminum, chrome and nickel, which can be found in moldings, surface coatings, furniture, lights, works of art or fittings, are all silver-colored. Their tones, along with their ability to reflect light, make them ideal for decorating theaters and night clubs.

Es importante considerar el peso que tiene en el interiorismo el color natural de los materiales pues, sea éste cual sea, necesariamente modifica la percepción del espacio que lo implique. Metales como el acero inoxidable, aluminio, cromo y níquel, que aparecen en la decoración en molduras, recubrimientos de superficies, mobiliario, luminarias, piezas artísticas o accesorios, tienen en común su coloración plata. Este color, aunado a su capacidad de reflejar la luz, hace de los metales materiales idóneos para decorar teatros, complejos de cine y centros nocturnos.

Lorsque l'on veut décorer un lieu, il est nécessaire de prendre en compte les couleurs des différents matériaux utilisés à l'état brut. Quelles que soient ces couleurs, elles modifient invariablement la perception que l'on se fait de l'endroit. Des métaux comme l'acier inoxydable, l'aluminium, le chrome et le nickel, couramment utilisés en décoration pour des moulures, des meubles, des luminaires, des créations artistiques, des accessoires et pour recouvrir certaines surfaces, sont tous de couleur argent. Cette teinte particulière à ces métaux, qui d'ailleurs reflète naturellement la lumière, est idéale pour des lieux publics comme les théâtres, les cinémas ou les boîtes de nuit.

Es ist wichtig, im Innendesign das Gewicht der Naturfarben von Materialien in Betracht zu ziehen, gleichgültig um welche es sich dabei handelt. Auf jeden Fall wird durch sie die Wahrnehmung des Raumes verändert. Metalle, wie rostfreier Edelstahl, Aluminium, Chrom und Nickel, die bei der Dekoration von Rahmen, Beschichtung von Oberflächen, Möbeln, Leuchten, Kunstwerken oder Accessoires Verwendung finden, sind alle silberfarbend. Diese Farbe spiegelt das Licht wider und eignet sich zur Dekoration von Theatern, Kinos und Nachtclubs.

bars bares

An effective method for separating the seating area from areas where people move from one place to another involves placing warm, bright colors in the middle with colder tones in the periphery.

Dejar todos los tonos cálidos y encendidos al centro y los fríos circundando el espacio conduce a delimitar la zona de convivencia de la de circulación.

Avec des teintes chaudes et vives au centre d'un endroit et des couleurs froides autour de la pièce, on sépare l'espace convivial des zones conçues pour se déplacer.

Verbleiben alle warmen und leuchtenden Farbtone in der Mitte und alle kullen um Rand, so wird der Bereich des Zusammenlebens von dem Durchgangsbereich abgegrenzt.

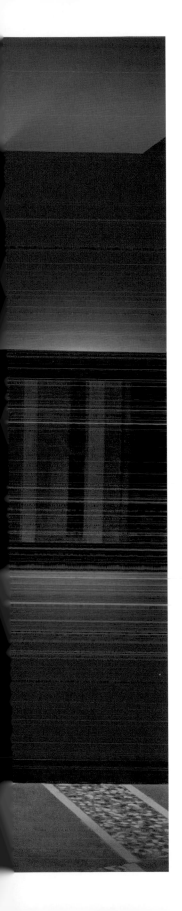

Creating a monochromatic setting probably seems an easy task, but choosing the color and its tones is not such a straightforward affair. If it's for a bar, then it should not be too dark or too light; it should be bright so that the shape and texture of all the different elements can be distinguished; and the lower and higher tones need to be balanced with the lighting to give the place visual continuity.

Sin duda, lograr un ambiente monocromático aparenta ser una alternativa sencilla, pero simplemente definir el color y sus tonalidades involucra muchas reflexiones. Si es para un bar no debe de ser ni muy oscuro ni muy claro; conviene que sea luminoso para que se puedan distinguir la forma y la textura de cada uno de los elementos de la composición; y que los tonos más bajos y más elevados estén en equilibrio con la iluminación, de modo que se pueda recorrer visualmente el lugar de principio a fin.

Opter pour une décoration monochrome paraît être sans aucun doute une solution facile à réussir. Pourtant, le choix de la couleur et de ses tons demande réflexion. Lorsque c'est pour un bar, la couleur ne doit être ni trop foncée, ni trop claire car il faut qu'elle apporte de la luminosité au lieu afin que l'on puisse distinguer la forme et la texture de chacun des éléments qui la composent. Il faut également qu'il y ait un certain équilibre entre, d'une part, les teintes les plus foncées et les plus vives et, d'autre part, l'éclairage pour que l'on soit à même de parcourir des yeux l'endroit dans son ensemble.

Ohne Zweifel scheint eine monochromatische Atmosphäre eine einfache Alternative zu sein, aber nur das Festlegen der Farbe und deren Abstufungen erfordert viele Überlegungen. Soll eine Farbe für eine Bar gewählt werden, darf diese weder sehr dunkel noch sehr hell sein. Am geeignetsten ist eine leuchtende Farbe, durch die die Formen und Texturen der einzelnen Elemento unterschieden werden können. Ferner sollten die dunkelsten und hellsten Töne im Einklang mit der Beleuchtung stehen, so dass der Raum vollständig überschaubar ist.

Translucent stone (and certain ceramics that imitate it) is an ideal choice for the bar, as the brightness of its colors and its veins are brought to life by the lighting to become visual focal points.

Las piedras translúcidas (y determinadas cerámicas que las imitan) son materiales perfectos para usarse en barras de bares, pues la intensidad de sus colores y veteado se reaviva al contacto con la luz, convirtiéndolas en puntos de atención que concentran el peso visual.

Les minéraux translucides (ainsi que certaines céramiques qui les imitent) sont des matériaux parfait pour le comptoir d'un bar. L'intensité des couleurs et les veines de la pierre sont mises en valeur par l'éclairage et le comptoir attire alors immanquablement les regards.

Transparente Steine (und bestimmte Keramikarten, die diesen ähneln) sind perfekte Materialien für Bars, denn die Intensität der Farben und ihrer Maserung werden durch das Licht verstärkt und verwandeln sie in zentrale Punkte, die alle Blicke auf sich ziehen.

Color can transform a common architectural element into a true protagonist and, by using the right proportions and composition, even turn it into a noteworthy sculptural object.

Con el color se puede provocar que un elemento arquitectónico común se convierta en protagonista del espacio y, cuidando bien la composición y las proporciones, incluso hacer de éste un interesante objeto escultórico.

En adoptant une certaine couleur, un élément architectural quelconque peut devenir l'objet décoratif le plus important de l'endroit. Si on soigne aussi sa composition et ses proportions, cela peut même devenir une sculpture intéressante.

Mit Farbe kann erreicht werden, dass ein gewöhnliches, architektonisches Element sich in den Hauptdarsteller des Raumes verwandelt und -sofern die Proportionen und die Zusammensetzung gelungen sind- kann es sogar zu einem interessanten, bildhauerischen Objekt werden.

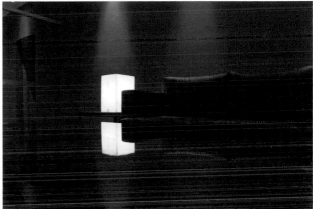

apartments apartamentos appartements wohnungen

Even though it is usually associated with bricks, the use of red on the front of an apartment block requires great care. To begin with, it is necessary to be aware of the difference between using color on a solid or blind wall and using it on one with openings. Windows, doors and any other architectural components that are left unpainted provide a visual break from color. If lively tones are used, then it is a good idea to study the proportions between solid surfaces and surfaces with openings.

A pesar de que se le relaciona con la apariencia del ladrillo, el uso del rojo en fachadas requiere de algunas recomendaciones. En primer instancia es conveniente entender que no es lo mismo la proporción de color en un muro macizo o ciego que en uno con vanos. Las ventanas, las puertas y cualquier otro componente de la arquitectura que no se pinte constituyen descansos visuales sin color. Sobre todo cuando se involucran matices enérgicos es muy útil analizar las proporciones entre macizos y vanos.

Décider de peindre la façade d'un bâtiment en rouge n'est pas chose si aisée. Bien que l'on associe cette couleur avec celle des briques, il convient de suivre quelques conseils. Car l'importance de la couleur n'est pas la même pour un mur aveugle (sans ouverture) et pour un mur qui comporte des fenêtres. Ces dernières, à l'instar des portes ou tout autre élément architectural qui ne se peint pas, permettent un certain repos pour les yeux. De plus, lorsque la couleur choisie est très vive, il est souhaitable de bien mesurer les proportions prises par la surface aveugle et par les ouvertures.

Obwohl die Farbe rot mit dem Aussehen von Ziegelsteinen in Verbindung gebracht wird, sollten bei ihrem Gebrauch einige Empfehlungen berücksichtigt werden. Zuerst muss verstanden werden, dass die Proportion in Bezug auf die Farbe einer massiven Wand nicht dieselbe einer Fassade mit Öffnungen ist. Fenster und Türen oder sonstige architektonische Komponenten, die nicht diese Farbe aufweisen, stellen visuelle Ruhepunkte ohne Farbe dar. Vor allem wenn energische Farbtöne verwendet werden ist es sehr nützlich, die Proportionen zwischen massiver Wand und Öffnungen zu analysieren.

schools
escuelas
établissements scolaires
schulen

Complementary color combinations such as blue-red and green-brown are tried and tested options, but are somewhat avant-garde when applied to schools.

Las combinaciones de colores complementarios azul-rojo y verde-café están muy probadas estéticamente, pero no dejan de ser vanguardistas si se trata de una escuela.

Les associations entre couleurs complémentaires bleu/rouge et vert/marron sont très classiques mais restent néanmoins très avant-gardistes pour un établissement scolaire.

Kombinationen von Komplementärfarben wie balu-rot und grün-braun sind ästhetisch sehr beliebt; im Falle einer Schule wirken sie sehr avantgardistisch.

It an architectural complex comprises different volumes, color can be used in alternation between one surface and another and only on certain architectural components.

Si un complejo arquitectónico se integra por varios volúmenes, se puede utilizar el color de manera alternada entre uno y otro cuerpo y sólo en determinados elementos de la arquitectura.

Si un ensemble architectural est composé par plusieurs éléments d'utiliser une couleur seulement pour certains d'entre eux et sur certaines parties.

Wenn ein architektonischer Komplex durch verschiedene Ebenen gekennzeichnet ist, kann die Farbe abwechselnd und nur an bestimmten Elementen der Architektur angebracht werden.

light
luz
lumière
licht

offices
oficinas
bureaux
büros

MOST OFFICES TODAY are flowing spaces that host a whole array of activities. This is why the first thing that needs to be resolved here is the general lighting, which must be functional and afford the visibility required for day-to-day duties. The ideal range is between 300 and 700 lx. Once the background lighting has been defined, we can move on to decorative aspects and more specific illumination.

LAS OFICINAS ACTUALES son, en su mayoría, espacios fluidos en los que se realizan múltiples actividades; por ello, lo primero que hay que solucionar es la iluminación general, cuidando que sea funcional y permita la visibilidad necesaria para ejercer las labores cotidianas. Los valores más adecuados van de los 300 a los 700 luxes. Una vez que se cuenta con este gran telón lumínico de fondo se puede trabajar en la parte decorativa y en puntualizaciones.

ON CONÇOIT LA PLUPART des bureaux aujourd'hui pour être des endroits où il est facile de circuler et où l'on peut procéder à l'exécution des tâches les plus variées. Il est donc important de bien en soigner l'éclairage général qui doit être à la fois fonctionnel et suffisant pour réaliser les tâches quotidiennes. L'intensité indiquée va en général de 300 à 700 lux. Une fois cet éclairage général obtenu, on peut réfléchir à la décoration et aux détails.

DIE DERZEITIGEN BÜROS sind meist durchgängige Bereiche, in denen verschiedenartige Tätigkeiten ausgeführt werden. Daher ist zuerst die allgemeine Beleuchtung zu lösen, wobei darauf zu achten ist, dass sie praktisch ist und alle Bereiche für die täglichen Arbeiten hell erleuchtet sind. Die angemessensten Werte gehen von 300 bis 700 Lux. Sobald die Beleuchtung angemessen eingerichtet wurde, kann der dekorative Teil begonnen werden, wobei auch spezielle Details zu berücksichtigen sind.

Daylight and artificial light bring out the contrasts between different surface textures.

Sea natural o artificial, uno de los potenciales de la luz es que permite diferenciar y resaltar las texturas de las superficies.

Qu'elle soit naturelle ou artificielle, un des atouts de la lumière réside dans le fait qu'elle permet de distinguer et de mettre en valeur la texture des différentes surfaces.

Gleichgültig ob natürlich oder künstlich: durch unterschiedliche Beleuchtung können die Strukturen der Oberflächen betont und hervorgehoben werden.

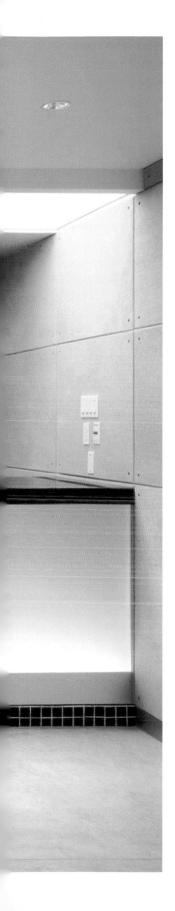

An eyestrain-free functional arrangement is the ultimate aim of strategically positioning artificial light sources. It is also important to make sure their spectrum is as similar as possible to daylight, as is the case with fluorescent light which is white and bright. If specific accents or focused lighting are required, then the angle of the lights' openings and the direction of the beams need to be controlled in accordance with the location of the light source. The tone also needs to be defined depending on how the light is to be used.

Para conseguir un diseño funcional y evitar el cansancio visual se debe procurar que las fuentes de iluminación artificial de las áreas de trabajo se ubiquen estratégicamente y que su espectro sea lo más similar al de la luz natural, como ocurre con el de la luz fluorescente que es blanca y brillante. Para acentos específicos o iluminación focalizada es necesario controlar el ángulo de apertura de las lámparas y la dirección de la luz según la posición de las luminarias y, dependiendo de su uso, definir específicamente su tono.

Lorsque l'on opte pour un design fonctionnel qui ne fatigue pas le regard, il est important de bien situer les sources de lumière artificielle dans les espaces de travail pour que le spectre lumineux ainsi créé ressemble le plus à celui de la lumière naturelle. C'est le cas de la lumière fluorescente, à la fois blanche et vive. Pour une lumière particulière, un éclairage dirigé, il faut régler l'angle d'ouverture des lampes et contrôler la direction de la lumière par rapport à l'emplacement des luminaires. Quant à la teinte de la lumière, cela dépend de l'usage que l'on veut en faire.

Für ein parktisches Design, das nicht zu einer visuellen Ermüdung führt, muss darauf geachtet werden, dass die künstlichen Lichtquellen an Arbeitsbereichen strategisch angebracht werden und dass ihr Spektrum dem von natürlichem Licht entspricht, so wie es bei Leuchtstoffröhren der Fall ist, die weisses und leuchtendes Licht abgeben. Zum Setzen von speziellen Akzenten oder bei speziell ausgerichteter Beleuchtung ist es erforderlich, den Öffnungswinkel der Leuchten und die Richtung des Lichtes zu kontrollieren, und dies in Übereinstimmung mit der Position der Lampen und ihrem Gebrauch, wobei dann auch ein spezifischer Farbton auszuwählen ist.

In corridors and passageways, light directed upwards or downwards helps bring out the sense of motion.

En pasillos y otros distribuidores la iluminación ascendente o descendente sirve para subrayar el recorrido de las circulaciones.

Un éclairage ascendant ou descendant est conseillé pour les couloirs et autres espaces de passage car il permet une bonne illumination de l'endroit que l'on parcourt.

In Gängen und Fluren dient auf- oder absteigendes Licht zum Abgrenzen der Wege.

Good decoration involves not just using different tones of light, but also experimenting with its intensity and effects for esthetic purpose. But it is also necessary to bear in mind that the primary role of office lighting is to ensure visual comfort. If perimeter or wall lighting is used, one good option for providing suitable illumination is hanging lamps.

Decorar no es sólo utilizar los diferentes tonos de la luz, sino también jugar con sus intensidades y efectos con fines estéticos. Pero no hay que dejar a un lado que la función primordial de la iluminación en oficinas es proveer de confort visual. Si dominan las luces perimetrales o las rasantes a muros, la solución son lámparas colgantes para iluminar eficazmente.

Décorer une pièce, ce n'est pas simplement utiliser les différents tons de la lumière. C'est aussi jouer sur l'intensité et les effets produits pour parvenir à un certain esthétisme. Toutefois, il ne faut pas oublier que l'éclairage dans des bureaux doit avant tout fournir un confort visuel. Si l'on se décide pour un éclairage périphérique ou rasant près des murs, des lampes suspendues constitueront la meilleure solution.

Die Dekoration beschäftigt sich nicht nur mit verschiedenen Farbtönen des Lichtes, sondern spielt auch mit dessen Intensität und Wirkung, um so ästhetische Zwecke zu erfüllen. Dabei ist nicht zu vergessen, dass die Funktion der Beleuchtung in Büros für den visuellen Komfort am wichtigsten ist. Dominieren perimetrale oder geneigte Lichter an den Wänden, kann durch die Verwendung von Hängelampen eine wirkungsvolle Beleuchtung erzielt werden.

restaurants
restaurantes

THE QUALITIES OF A GIVEN LIGHTING ARRANGEMENT and the way it adapts to the different spatial needs and tastes of clients can affect a restaurant's success. It is therefore advisable to offer different atmospheres in the same place with a specific lighting scheme for each one. In the bar area, for instance, the lighting should help create a lively ambience while in the dining area it should not distort the color of the food.

LOS ATRIBUTOS DEL DISEÑO DE ILUMINACIÓN así como su adaptación a las necesidades del espacio y a los gustos del cliente pueden repercutir en el éxito de un restaurante. Por ello, en un mismo local es útil contar con diversos ambientes y desarrollar un esquema lumínico para cada uno de ellos. En el bar, por ejemplo, es importante que el clima lumínico sea candente, pero en el comedor la iluminación debe ser cuidada para que no distorsione el color de los alimentos.

LES PARTICULARITÉS DE L'ÉCLAIRAGE, le fait qu'il soit pratique et qu'il corresponde aux goûts des clients, peut contribuer au succès d'un restaurant. Il est donc conseillé d'avoir recourt à plusieurs types d'éclairages dans un même établissement afin de créer différentes atmosphères. Par exemple, dans la partie bar, la lumière doit être chaude, alors que dans la salle de restaurant elle ne doit pas être trop intense pour ne pas altérer la couleur des aliments.

DAS DESIGN DER BELEUCHTUNG sowie dessen Anpassung an die Erfordernisse des Raumes und die Vorlieben der Kunden, können Auswirkungen auf den Erfolg eines Restaurants haben. Daher ist es nützlich, wenn an ein und demselben Ort verschiedene Atmosphären vorhanden sind und jede Einzelne über eine spezifische Beleuchtung verfügt. In einer Bar ist es zum Beispiel wichtig, dass das Beleuchtungsklima glühend ist. Hingegen wird im Essbereich ein Licht benötigt, das die Farben der Nahrungsmittel nicht verfälscht.

A wonderful decorative effect can be achieved in long, narrow spaces by creating two linear, light-differentiated strips. It's also very easy to do. Warm-colored light is used on one side with colder, white light on the other. The former will generate a cozy atmosphere, while the latter makes for a more intense and paler ambience. This appealing contrast can be accentuated by using color in the same direction, which means positioning it in accordance with the tone of the light and making it match the temperature.

Crear dos franjas lineales y diferenciadas de luz es un recurso decorativo excepcional para espacios largos y angostos, además de ser sencillo de implementar. En un lado se colocan fuentes que emiten luz cálida y en el otro las de luz fría y blanca. Con las primeras se consigue una atmósfera acogedora y con las segundas un ambiente intenso y claro. Este llamativo contraste se refuerza con el uso del color en el mismo sentido, es decir, ubicándolo por afinidad con el tono de la luz y, por lo tanto, coincidiendo con su temperatura.

Pour des pièces longues et étroites, deux bandes de lumière d'intensité différente donneront un effet exceptionnel. C'est, de plus, simple à installer. Dans un côté de la pièce, on place un éclairage chaud et, dans l'autre, on choisit une illumination froide et de couleur blanche. D'un côté, on obtient donc une atmosphère qui donne la sensation d'être dans un endroit confortable. De l'autre côté, on a l'impression de se trouver dans un lieu très clair où l'activité est intense. On peut renforcer les effets de cette opposition en jouant sur les couleurs avec des éclairages en adéquation avec les teintes choisies et par conséquent, avec l'atmosphère de la salle.

Zwei längliche, unterschiedliche Streifen mit Licht sind ausserordentliche, dekorative und leicht umsetzbare Lösungen für lange, schmale Bereiche. Auf einer Seite werden warme Lichtquellen angebracht und auf der anderen Seite weisses, kaltes Licht. Erstere führen zu einer gemütlichen Atmosphäre und letzteres zu einer intensiven und klaren Atmosphäre. Dieser auffällige Kontrast wird durch die Verwendung von Farbe mit demselben Effekt noch verstärkt, das heisst, der Farbton entspricht dem Licht und stimmt mit dessen Temperatur überein.

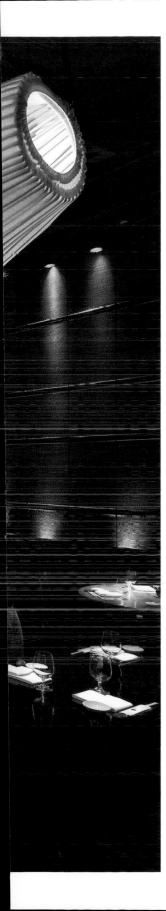

In addition to the light, the lamps themselves can play a leading decorative role, especially if they are sizeable. In a Japanese restaurant, for example, light from two large lamps cuts lengthwise through the space to become the area's main feature.

No solamente la luz sino también las lámparas se pueden convertir en el eje decorativo de un lugar, sobre todo si la escala de éstas es imponente. En un restaurante japonés, por ejemplo, dos lámparas de grandes proporciones que atraviesan longitudinalmente el espacio se vuelven sus principales habitantes.

La lumière est bien sûr l'élément-clé de la décoration dans un espace donné mais c'est aussi le cas des lampes, surtout si celles-ci sont de taille imposante. On voit dans ce restaurant japonais, par exemple, deux énormes lampes qui traversent toute la pièce dans sa longueur et qui en deviennent l'accessoire décoratif le plus important.

Nicht nur das Licht, sondern auch die Lampen können sich in die dekorative Achse eines Ortes verwandeln, vor allem, wenn die Ausmasse der Räume gross sind. In einem japanischen Restaurant werden zum Beispiel zwei grosse Lampen zum Mittelpunkt, die längs den Raum durchqueren.

Lighting will be sufficient for cellars if
it is cold and comes from low-power,
scattered light sources.

Hoy las cavas pueden tener suficiente
luz si ésta es fría y procede de
focos de luz dispersa y poca potencia.

Il est possible aujourd'hui d'éclairer
suffisamment une cave avec une lumière
froide et des ampoules bien éloignées les
unes des autres et peu intenses.

Heute können Weinkeller ausreichend
Licht aufweisen, sofern es sich um
kalte Beleuchtung handelt, die aus
Glühlampen mit gestreutem Licht und
wenig Leistung stammt.

Leds are a great option for emitting high yield, low-consumption colored light. These diodes can actually infuse the atmosphere with color as an almost ethereal presence, which is precisely why the range of decorative possibilities they offer restaurants and bars, where this kind of effect works especially well, is endless. But it is also necessary to remember that, in addition to light, color is also involved, which means there are rules to bear in mind. Blue and green, for example, are cold and need to be balanced by something a little warmer.

Los Leds son un invento extraordinario para emitir luz de color con rendimiento luminoso elevado y bajo consumo energético. Con estos diodos es literalmente posible teñir un ambiente y sentir el color de una forma elérea, por ello, sus posibilidades en la decoración de restaurantes y bares, donde estas ambientaciones van estupendas, son infinitas. Sin embargo, no hay que perder de vista que aunque se trate de luz también está implicado el color, por lo que es importante considerar sus reglas. Por ejemplo, el azul y el verde requieren equilibrar su frialdad con elementos cálidos.

Les Leds sont une invention extraordinaire pour un éclairage coloré de forte intensité mais à faible consommation d'électricité. Grâce à ces fameuses diodes, il est littéralement possible de teindre l'espace pour donner l'impression de se déplacer dans un univers éthéré. L'usage que l'on peut faire des Leds dans le domaine de la décoration pour un restaurant ou un bar est donc infini. Bien que l'on parle ici de lumière, il ne faut pas oublier la couleur et respecter quelques règles. Le froid dégagé par les lumières verte ou bleue doit ainsi être compensé par certains éléments apportant de la chaleur.

Leuchtdioden sind eine aussergewöhnliche Erfindung, die buntes Licht abgeben und hohe Leuchtleistungen erreichen, wobei nur wenig Energie benötigt wird. Mit diesen Dioden kann eine Atmosphäre regelrecht gefärbt und die Farbe als etwas Ätherisches wahrgenommen werden. Daher sind die dekorativen Möglichkeiten in Restaurants und Bars unendlich und führen zu attraktiven Ergebnissen. Dennoch darf nicht vernachlässigt werden, dass es sich nicht nur um Licht handelt, sondern auch um Farbe, daher ist es wichtig, die Regeln einzuhalten. So muss zum Beispiel die Kälte der Farben blau und grün durch warme Elemente ausgeglichen werden.

If the sources of lighting are hidden inside architectural or decorative components or are part of them, an air of mystique can be generated. Soffits, onyx slabs and bar furniture, among other things, are particularly good for creating such an effect.

Cuando las fuentes de luz se ocultan entre y/o se integran a los diversos elementos arquitectónicos y decorativos se genera un misterio visual único; para ello son útiles, entre otros, plafones, planchas de ónix y muebles de bar.

Lorsque les sources de lumière sont dissimulées par divers éléments architecturaux et décoratifs ou lorsqu'elles en font tellement partie qu'on ne les remarque plus, l'éclairage devient alors un mystère qu'il est difficile de résoudre. Pour profiter d'une telle disposition, on se servira des faux plafonds, des panneaux lumineux en onyx et du mobilier du bar.

Wenn die Lichtquellen zwischen verschiedenen architektonischen und dekorativen Elementen verborgen und/oder in dieselben integriert werden, so wird ein einzigartiges visuelles Mysterium geschaffen. Dafür sind unter anderem abgehängte Decken, Onyxplatten und Barmöbel geeignet.

For a more formal restaurant, the general lighting should be subtle and uniform. This can be done by concealing the source of light in wall sections and soffits from where they shoot sleek rays of white light into the surroundings. If the space is big enough, a touch of stylishness can be achieved with luminous volumes similar in size to the furniture; but for smaller places light sources placed in the middle of the tables will do the trick. A sensual and pleasurable atmosphere is generated for diners.

Si se trabaja en la iluminación de un restaurante formal conviene seleccionar una luz tenue y uniforme para el ambiente general y esconder en cajillos de muros y plafones fuentes luminosas que irradien esbeltas líneas de luz blanca. Para dar el toque, cuando la dimensión del espacio lo permite, se sugieren cuerpos lumínicos a escala del mobiliario; pero si el sitio es pequeño es suficiente con puntos luminosos colocados al centro de las mesas. La atmósfera que se genera es sensual e invoca en los comensales sensaciones placenteras.

En ce qui concerne l'éclairage d'un restaurant élégant, on optera pour une lumière réduite et uniforme pour l'ensemble des lieux et on dissimulera dans les murs et les faux-plafonds des sources de lumière projetant de fins rayons de lumière blanche. Le petit détail qui fait la différence, lorsque les dimensions de l'endroit le permettent : des appareils d'éclairage dont la taille est proportionnelle à celle du mobilier. Mais lorsque le site est de dimension réduite, quelques sources lumineuses au centre des tables suffiront. L'atmosphère créée est alors très sensuelle et le bien-être règne parmi les convives.

Soll ein formelles Restaurant mit Beleuchtung ausgestattet werden, ist es angebracht ein dezentes, gleichmässiges Licht für die allgemeine Atmosphäre zu wählen. In Wandnischen und abgehängten Decken können dann Lichtquellen angebracht werden, die zierliche Linien aus weissem Licht ausstrahlen. Für einen besonderen Touch, können Leuchtkörper von der Grösse der Möbel aufgestellt werden, sofern dies das Ausmass des Raumes erlaubt. In kleinen Räumen ist es ausreichend, Leuchtpunkte zu setzen, die in der Mitte der Tische angebracht werden. Die geschaffene Atmosphäre ist sinnlich und ruft bei den Essensgästen angenehme Empfindungen hervor.

The ambient lighting of a large lounge/dining room needs to be encircling, subtle and scattered at the same time. It can be accentuated by using hanging lamps that emit stronger light. This option is ideal for highlighting the decorative accents, textures, colors and shapes of the furniture and fittings.

La iluminación ambiental de un gran salón-comedor debe ser envolvente, sutil y difusa. Se le puede reforzar con lámparas colgantes de luz más intensa. Estos cambios de luz funcionan muy bien para acentuar los acentos decorativos, así como las texturas, colores y formas tanto del mobiliario como de los accesorios.

L'éclairage général de la salle principale d'un restaurant doit être enveloppant, discret et diffus. Si l'on souhaite en augmenter un peu l'intensité, des lampes suspendues projetant une lumière plus vive suffiront. Ces ajouts lumineux sont très utiles lorsque l'on désire mettre en relief certains aspects de la décoration, comme les textures, les couleurs et les formes du mobilier ou des accessoires.

Die Beleuchtung der Atmosphäre eines grossen Eßsaales sollte einhüllend, raffiniert und diffus sein. Dies kann durch Hängelampen mit intensiverem Licht verstärkt werden. Diese Lichtwechsel sind besonders zum Hervorheben von dekorativen Akzenten, sowie Strukturen, Farben und Formen der Möbel und Accesoires geeignet.

stores
tiendas
boutiques
geschäfte

THE MAIN CHALLENGE when it comes to choosing a lighting scheme for stores is to highlight the qualities of the different products but without causing any damage to them if they are sensitive to light, especially UV. Designers are keen on high-precision, concentrated-beam halogen lamps for lighting up specific points and turning the illuminated item into a work of art.

AL ILUMINAR TIENDAS se tiene como principal reto realzar los atributos de los productos y reducir al máximo los daños que éstos puedan sufrir cuando son sensibles a la luz, especialmente a la ultravioleta. Es común que los diseñadores utilicen lámparas halógenas de alta precisión y haz concentrado para alcanzar una iluminación puntual y convertir al objeto iluminado casi en una pieza museística susceptible de ser admirada.

LE PRINCIPAL PROBLÈME posé par l'éclairage des boutiques réside dans le fait qu'il faille mettre en relief les produits à vendre sans les abîmer car ils sont souvent sensibles à la lumière, en particulier aux ultraviolets. Pour parvenir à relever ce défi, les designers ont généralement recours à des lampes halogènes de haute précision et avec un faisceau lumineux dirigé. Le produit éclairé se transforme alors presque en pièce de musée que l'on peut admirer.

BEI DER BELEUCHTUNG VON GESCHÄFTEN ist das Hauptziel das Hervorheben der Produkte, wobei darauf zu achten ist, dass Schäden an lichtempfindlichen Artikeln soweit wie möglich vermieden werden; dies gilt besonders für Ware, die empfindlich auf ultraviolettes Licht reagiert. Für gewöhnlich verwenden die Designer präzise Halogenlampen mit konzentriertem Lichtstrahl, um eine punktuelle Beleuchtung zu erzielen. So wird der beleuchtete Artikel fast zu einem Museumsstück, das die Blicke auf sich zieht.

Double height stores can be decorated by integrating the lighting of both levels to achieve a sense of unity; a good bet for creating this kind of effect is lamps that scatter light and color uniformly. The atmosphere is completed with lighting that brings out the qualities of the items on sale. In the case of a clothes store, the advantage of fluorescent lamps providing "daylight" lighting is that their light is continuous (very similar to daylight), which emphasizes the textures and colors of the different garments without damaging them.

En espacios comerciales de doble altura una posibilidad decorativa es integrar la iluminación de ambos niveles para que se perciba un clima unitario; son útiles para estos fines las luminarias que garantizan dispersión uniforme de la luz y rendimiento del color. La atmósfera se completa con luminarias que destaquen las propiedades de los artículos en venta. Para el caso de tiendas de ropa, las lámparas fluorescentes tipo "luz día" ofrecen la ventaja de proporcionar luz continua (muy similar a la natural), resaltando las texturas y coloridos de las prendas, sin dañarlas.

Pour les boutiques à deux étages, il est possible d'utiliser le même éclairage pour les deux niveaux afin d'uniformiser l'ensemble. Les luminaires qui garantissent un éclairage et une tonalité uniformes sont tout indiqués pour y parvenir. A l'atmosphère ainsi créée, on peut y ajouter d'autres luminaires qui mettront en valeur les articles en vente. Lorsqu'il s'agit d'une boutique de vêtements, des lampes fluorescentes avec des ampoules « lumière du jour » sont conseillées car la lumière projetée est constante, très proche de la lumière naturelle et fait ressortir les textures et les coloris des vêtements sans les abîmer.

In Einkaufszentren mit doppelter Deckenhöhe ist eine dekorative Möglichkeit die Integration von Beleuchtung auf beiden Ebenen, denn so wird eine einheitliche Atmosphäre geschaffen. Dafür sind besonders Leuchten geeignet, die eine gleichmässige Streuung des Lichtes und eine gleichmässige Farbleistung sicherstellen. Die Atmosphäre wird durch Lampen vervollständigt, die die Eigenschaften der zum Kauf angebotenen Artikel hervorheben. Im Fall von Bekleidungsgeschäften sind Leuchtstoffröhren vom Typ "Tageslicht" vorteilhaft, die ein gleichmässiges Licht liefern, das dem des Tageslichtes ähnelt. Dabei werden die Texturen und Farben der Stücke hervorgehoben, ohne sie zu beschädigen.

miscellaneous locations
espacios diversos
lieux divers
verschiedene bereiche

shopping malls
centros comerciales
centres commerciaux
einkaufszentren

Lighting in a shopping mall should be pleasant enough to entice shoppers to spend more time there and provide maximum visual comfort. Daylight filtered through domes and transparent elements is definitely the best daytime option for illuminating large areas and keeping energy bills down. Heat can be kept to a minimum by the use of effective daylight filters, and the shadows generated in the space create an appealing effect.

Se espera que la iluminación de un centro comercial no sólo sea agradable e invite a los visitantes a permanecer en el sitio, sino que ofrezca un nivel de confort visual óptimo. La luz natural captada a través de domos y transparencias es, desde luego, la mejor alternativa durante el día para alumbrar grandes áreas y abatir los costos de energía. La carga térmica se puede abatir con partesoles efectivos, además, las sombras que produce en el espacio son altamente atractivas.

L'éclairage dans un centre commercial ne doit bien sûr pas être agressif pour que les clients n'hésitent pas à y rester longtemps. Mais l'endroit doit aussi être parfaitement éclairé. La lumière naturelle, grâce à un toit vitré ou d'autres éléments transparents, est évidemment idéale pendant la journée pour de grandes surfaces et pour diminuer la facture énergétique. La chaleur émise parfois par ces structures peut être contrôlée grâce à des brise-soleil. Qui plus est, les ombres apportées par ces derniers sont très esthétiques.

Von der Beleuchtung eines Einkaufszentrums wird nicht nur erwartet, dass sie angenehm ist und die Besucher zum Verbleib an diesem Ort einläd, sondern sie soll auch einen optimalen, visuellen Komfort bieten. Natürliches Licht, das durch Oberlichter und transparente Bereiche einfällt ist natürlich die beste Alternative, um tagsüber grosse Bereiche zu erhellen und gleichzeitig Stromkosten zu sparen. Die Hitze, die durch den Sonneneinfall entsteht, kann durch effektive Sonnenblenden abgewendet werden. Ausserdem sind die so erzeugten Schatten äusserst attraktiv.

movie theaters
cines
cinémas
kinos

The industrial design of lights for different types of theaters relies on their shapes, the qualities of the light they produce and the direction of their beam to produce a magical setting while avoiding saturated light.

En el diseño industrial de luminarias para cines y teatros cuentan tanto la forma de éstas como las calidades de luz y la dirección de su haz para llegar a un clima mágico, evitando la saturación lumínica.

La production industrielle de luminaires pour cinémas et théâtres doit soigner aussi bien la forme des objets que la qualité de la lumière et la direction du faisceau. Car le but est de créer un climat magique en évitant les lumières saturées.

In Bezug auf das industrielle Design von Beleuchtung für Kinos und Theater, sind sowohl die Form derselben als auch die Lichtqualität sowie die Richtung des Lichtstrahls entscheidend für eine magische Atmosphäre, wobei eine Übersättigung an Licht zu vermeiden ist.

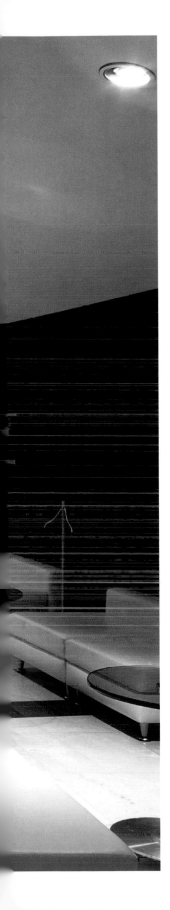

In the case of movie theatres, the use of light depends on the design, which determines every aspect of the space. A theatre lobby can cater for more than one protagonist, so a number of large, well-planned and elaborate lights can be used as exhibition items, generating different effects and affording an element of flow.

En el caso de los cines el manejo de la luz es un elemento de diseño, pues a través de ella cambia todo cuanto está en el espacio. Un lobby de cine admite más de un protagonista, así que se puede introducir varias luminarias de buen tamaño pensadas y elaboradas como piezas de exhibición, cuyos efectos luminosos sean variados y doten de movilidad al lugar.

En ce qui concerne les cinémas, l'éclairage est un des éléments à part entière du design général car il modifie complètement l'aspect de tout ce qui s'y trouve. Le hall d'entrée peut être éclairé de plusieurs façons simultanées. On peut donc y placer divers luminaires de taille importante qui seront pensés et conçus pour être considérés comme des œuvres d'art et la lumière produite sera variée et donnera du mouvement à l'espace.

Im Falle von Kinos ist die Beleuchtung ein Element des Designs, denn durch das Licht verändert sich der gesamte Raum. Der Eingangsbereich eines Kinos lässt mehr als einen Hauptdarsteller zu, so dass sogar mehrere Leuchten mit grossen Ausmassen und auffälligem Design gewählt werden können, deren Beleuchtungseffekte verschieden sein können und dem Raum Bewegung verleihen.

apartments
apartamentos
appartements
wohnungen

The most important thing when it comes to lighting up a terrace is the combination of daylight and artificial light, including special attention for the swimming pool, corridors, split levels and rest areas.

Lo más relevante del diseño de iluminación de una terraza es equilibrar la mezcla lumínica artificial y natural, así como destacar las zonas de alberca, pasillos, cambios de niveles y descansos.

Le plus important pour le design de l'éclairage d'une terrasse réside dans l'équilibre que l'on doit trouver entre lumières naturelle et artificielle et dans le fait qu'il faille mettre en valeur la piscine, les couloirs, les différents niveaux du sol (marches et surfaces planes).

Das Wichtigste beim Beleuchtungsdesign einer Terrasse ist das Gleichgewicht zwischen künstlichem und natürlichem Licht, sowie die Betonung von Schwimmbädern, Gängen, unterschiedlichen Ebenen und Absätzen.

Three basic factors need to be borne in mind when illuminating the outdoor areas of a residence: look, safety and comfort. One way to cater for these requirements is by positioning several low level lights at different locations, avoiding dark areas and ramping up the visibility in entrances, passageways and the building number. To give this option a real touch of style, you can generate a gentle contrast between the warmth of the general ambience and a few accents of cold light on certain perimeters. This combination will make the space more appealing.

Al pensar en iluminar el exterior de una residencia conviene que hacer confluir tres objetivos: estética, seguridad y confort. Un procedimiento posible es incluir en el proyecto varias luminarias de bajo nivel de iluminación, a lo largo y ancho del sitio, evitando zonas de penumbras, y favoreciendo la visibilidad en accesos, circulaciones, numeración del edificio. Para que el efecto sea más decorativo está la opción de crear una suave tensión entre la calidez del clima general y algunos acentos de luz fría en determinados perímetros. Esta combinación proporciona un grado de interés al espacio.

Lorsque l'on réfléchit à l'éclairage extérieur d'un appartement, il faut toujours garder à l'esprit trois éléments : l'esthétique, la sécurité et le confort. Une façon de parvenir à concilier ces trois objectifs consiste à prévoir plusieurs luminaires à éclairage réduit disposés un peu partout dans l'espace. On évite ainsi les zones de pénombre et on améliore la visibilité des entrées, des sorties et des lieux de passage et les numéros des bâtiments sont bien visibles. On peut aussi soigner la décoration en jouant sur une légère opposition entre une atmosphère générale plutôt chaude et quelques touches froides de lumière à certains endroits. Cette association rehausse l'intérêt que l'on peut porter au lieu.

Bei der Beleuchtung des Aussenbereiches eines Wohnhauses, sollten folgende Aspekte Berücksichtigung finden: Ästhetik, Sicherheit und Komfort. Eine mögliche Vorgehensweise ist der Einbezug von schwacher Beleuchtung an den Quer- und Längsseiten des Ortes, wobei dunkle Zonen zu vermeiden sind und besonders die Zugänge, Durchgänge und die Hausnummer hell erleuchtet sein sollten. Damit dies noch dekorativer aussieht, kann eine weiche Spannung zwischen der Wärme des allgemeinen Klimas und einigen Akzenten aus kaltem Licht an bestimmten Stellen geschaffen werden. Diese Kombination macht den Bereich interessanter.

The aim of any lighting scheme for the front of a building is to bring out its full splendor. If the surface has many openings, as opposed to being solid and uninterrupted, the central theme of the scheme will be the openings themselves, because they will become light boxes by night and take in sunlight during the day.

La iluminación de una fachada debe de estar orientada a sacar el máximo partido al exterior de una construcción. Cuando los vanos predominan sobre los macizos, los primeros se convierten en el tema central de la iluminación, pues por la noche lucen como cajas de luz y en el día captan luz natural al interior.

L'éclairage d'une façade doit être conçu pour mettre le plus en valeur l'extérieur du bâtiment.
Si la surface occupée par les fenêtres et autres ouvertures est plus importante que celle du mur, l'éclairage devra souligner leur présence. La nuit, elles ressembleront à des écrins lumineux et le jour elles capteront la lumière naturelle pour la diriger vers l'intérieur.

Die Beleuchtung einer Fassade sollte darauf ausgerichtet sein, den Aussenbereich eines Hauses so vorteilhaft wie eben möglich darzustellen. Wenn mehr Öffnungen als massive Bereiche vorhanden sind, werden erstere zum zentralen Thema der Beleuchtung, da sie in der Nacht aussehen wie Lampen und tagsüber das natürliche Licht ins Innere gelangen lassen.

The qualities of light and shade offer good options for illuminating areas used for funerals, where the main objective is to create a mood of serenity. This can be achieved by using hidden light sources and focused beams.

El claroscuro exalta los atributos de la luz y la sombra. Se presta muy bien para resolver la iluminación de espacios destinados a rituales fúnebres, en donde lo que se pretende es composiciones que evoquen serenidad. Esto se logra con luces ocultas y manipulando haces de luz concentrada.

Le clair-obscur fait ressortir les qualités de la lumière et de l'ombre. Idéal pour l'éclairage des endroits où l'on procède à des obsèques, le clair-obscur est indispensable pour un éclairage qui se veut solennel. On parvient à cet effet grâce à des sources des lumières dissimulées et des faisceaux lumineux de forte intensité et bien dirigés.

Das Helldunkel betont die Attribute von Licht und Schatten. Es eignet sich besonders zur Beleuchtung von Bereichen, die Bestattungsritualen vorenthalten sind, an denen Kompositionen angestrebt werden, die einen Eindruck von Ruhe erwecken. Dies kann durch verdeckte Leuchten und konzentrierte Lichtbündel erreicht werden.

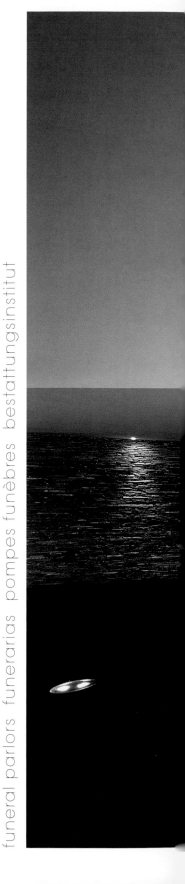

funeral parlors funerarias pompes funèbres bestattungsinstitut

A sense of solemnity can be generated through soft, delicate lighting that is conducive to relaxation and intimacy. Low intensity lighting will help create a soothing ambience. Blue lighting will infuse the area with peacefulness, while warmer tones provide an atmosphere of protection and sanctuary.

La noción de solemnidad en un lugar se consigue con una iluminación suave y delicada que invite a la relajación y evoque intimidad. Mantener la luz a baja intensidad coopera a conseguir un ambiente sedante. Una atmósfera azul crea la sensación de que la paz recorre el espacio, en tanto que las tonalidades cálidas hacen sentir cobijo y amparo.

Il est possible de faire d'un endroit un lieu solennel grâce à un éclairage réduit et délicat qui invite à l'apaisement et à l'intimité. On peut créer cette atmosphère propice au calme avec une lumière peu intense. Si l'on opte pour une lumière bleutée, on aura l'impression que la paix caractérise cet endroit alors que les tonalités plus chaudes donnent une impression plus rassurante.

Der Eindruck von Besinnlichkeit an einem Ort wird durch ein weiches, feines Licht erzielt, die zur Entspannung einläd und Privatsphäre schafft. Eine abgedunkelte Beleuchtung führt zu einer beruhigenden Atmosphäre. Blaues Licht erweckt den Eindruck von Frieden und warme Farben bieten Geborgenheit und Schutz.

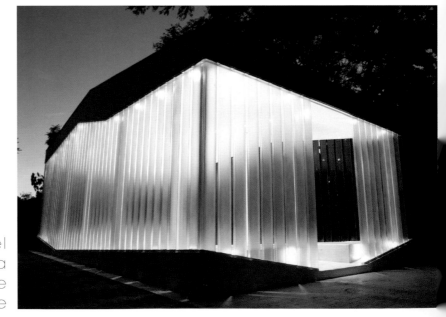

chapel
capilla
chapelle
kapelle

When translucent materials are correctly illuminated, they will transform the sense of spaciousness in accordance with the amount and quality –natural or artificial– of light provided at any given time.

Al ser iluminados, los materiales translúcidos modifican la sensación del espacio según sea la calidad y cantidad de luz –natural o artificial– que reciban en cada momento.

Les matériaux translucides, s'ils sont éclairés, modifient l'atmosphère de l'endroit mais tout dépend de la qualité et de la quantité de la lumière (naturelle ou artificielle) reçue.

Durch die Beleuchtung, verändern die durchscheinenden Materialien den Eindruck des Raumes, und dies in Abhängigkeit von Qualität und Quantität des Lichtes, wobei auch entscheidend ist, ob es sich um natürliches oder künstliches Licht handelt.

health clubs spas clubs de remise en forme gesundheitsclubs

Light is a vital factor for decorating the area containing the bathtub or jacuzzi. The best bet is to make the most of daylight by toning its intensity with elements in the ceiling and walls that will scatter it accordingly. Artificial light can also be toned to create a relaxing effect on the surfaces, textures and decorative materials. Translucent onyx screens can provide some wonderful effects by placing the sources of light behind them. Polished surfaces in the bathroom are an ideal way to reflect light.

La luz es de fundamental importancia en la decoración del área de tina y/o jacuzzi, donde se sugiere aprovechar la iluminación natural, matizando su fuerza con difusores tanto en techo como en muros. Las fuentes de luz artificial deben también ser matizadas para que sus efectos sobre superficies, texturas y materiales utilizados en la decoración inviten a la relajación. Las pantallas translúcidas de ónix a las que se les coloca lámparas traseras proveen impresiones luminosas interesantes. En el área específica de aseo y arreglo las superficies muy pulidas reflejan mejor la luz.

La lumière est un élément fondamental pour la décoration de la pièce où se trouve la baignoire et/ou le jacuzzi. Il est recommandé de profiter de la lumière naturelle en nuançant son intensité avec des diffuseurs au plafond comme sur les murs. La lumière artificielle doit également être nuancée pour que les textures et les matériaux utilisés dans la décoration, lorsqu'ils sont éclairés, contribuent à faire de la pièce un endroit propice à la détente. Les effets lumineux créés par des panneaux translucides en onyx, avec des lampes placées derrière, sont intéressants. Pour les endroits spécialement conçus pour l'hygiène et les soins de beauté, on suggérera des surfaces très bien polies car elles reflètent mieux la lumière.

Das Licht ist von besonderer Bedeutung bei der Dekoration der Badewannen und/oder Whirlpools, die vorwiegend mit natürlichem Licht beleuchtet werden sollten, wobei die Lichtstärke mit Diffusoren an Decke und Wänden abgemildert werden kann. Auch die bei der Dekoration verwendeten künstlichen Lichtquellen müssen abgemildert werden, damit deren Effekte auf Oberflächen, Strukturen und Materialien zur Entspannung einladen. Durchscheinende Onyxflächen, hinter denen Lampen angebracht werden, führen zu interessanten Beleuchtungseindrücken. In den Bereichen, die speziell der Hygiene und Schönheit vorenthalten sind, reflektieren hochpolierte Oberflächen das Licht besser.

The lighting in a spa's waiting and relaxation areas should not be overwhelming, but rather provide warmth and a decorative touch. It is a good idea to have full control over the sources of light in such places, because each client will have his or her preferences with regard to the lighting.

En las áreas de espera y relajación de un spa la iluminación no tiene que ser profusa, sino cálida y con intenciones decorativas. El control total de la intensidad de las luminarias en estos ambientes es muy útil, sobre todo porque cada cliente tiene sus preferencias lumínicas.

Dans un spa, les pièces destinées à l'attente et à la
relaxation doivent à peine être éclairées mais la lumière doit
rester chaude et contribuer à la décoration de l'espace.
Pouvoir pleinement contrôler l'intensité lumineuse est fort
utile car chaque habitué de l'endroit a des préférences
bien définies en matière d'éclairage

In den Warte- und Entspannungsbereichen des Spas ist eine
gemässigte, warme Beleuchtung angebracht, die dekorative
Absichten erfüllt. Die vollständige Kontrolle der Beleuchtung in
diesen Atmosphären ist sehr nützlich, vor allem, weil jeder Kunde
seine eigenen Vorlieben in Bezug auf die Beleuchtung hat.

beauty salon
salón de belleza
salon de beauté
schönheitssalon

Incandescent lights should be kept away from mirrors and make-up areas, where fluorescent light is preferable.

Las luminarias incandescentes deben quedar lejos de espejos y zonas de maquillaje, donde debe haber luces fluorescentes.

Les luminaires incandescents doivent être situés loin des miroirs et des endroits où l'on procède au maquillage. Pour ces zones bien délimitées, on optera pour un éclairage à base d'ampoules fluorescentes.

Glühlampen müssen weit entfernt von Spiegeln und Schminkbereichen angebracht werden, an denen Leuchtstoffröhren verwendet werden sollten.

IMPOSIBLE ES SOLO UNA PALABRA QUE USAN LOS HOMBRES DÉBILES FACILMENTE EN EL MUNDO QUE SE LES DIO, SIN ATREVERSE A EXPLORAR EL PODER QUE TIENEN PARA CAMBIARLO. IMPOSIBLE NO ES UN HECHO, ES UNA OPINIÓN. IMPOSIBLE NO ES UNA DECLARACIÓN, ES UN RETO.. IMPOSIBLE ES POTENCIAL. IMPOSIBLE ES TEMPORAL.

IMPOSSIBLE IS NOTHING.

offices oficinas bureaux büros

THE KIND OF WORK people do in an office should be borne in mind when choosing its design. One good way to make the most of the available space is to leave the floor as free as possible, avoiding columns and non-structural floor-to-ceiling walls, and using modular furniture. The aim is to ensure enough flexibility to increase or reduce spaces at a subsequent stage, rearrange furniture or redistribute areas without too much effort.

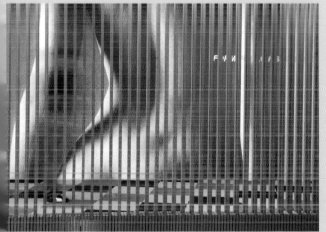

SEGÚN LAS LABORES que se lleven a cabo en una oficina, conviene plantear de una u otra manera su diseño. Para aprovechar el espacio, lo mejor es dejar la planta lo más libre posible, evitar columnas y muros de piso a techo que no sean estructurales y amueblar con modulares. Con ello se consigue la flexibilidad para posteriormente ampliar o reducir zonas, reacomodar mobiliario o redistribuir áreas sin tener que hacer grandes obras.

LE DESIGN D'UN BUREAU doit être pensé en fonction des tâches qui s'y exécutent. Il est conseillé de profiter au maximum de l'espace en évitant les ajouts inutiles tel que des colonnes ou des murs du sol au plafond lorsque ces éléments ne font pas partie de la structure de l'ensemble. On suggérera également des meubles facilement adaptables à toutes les pièces. Avec ce type de mobilier que l'on place où l'on veut, on peut facilement modifier l'ensemble des locaux et agrandir ou réduire des pièces sans pour autant avoir besoin d'entreprendre d'énormes travaux.

IN ÜBEREINSTIMMUNG MIT DEN ARBEITEN, die in einem Büro verrichtet werden, muss auch das Design geplant werden. Um den Raum gut auszunutzen, sollte der Boden so frei wie möglich bleiben, wobei Säulen und Mauern vom Boden bis zur Decke zu vermeiden sind, sofern sie nicht tragend sind. Als Möbel sind Module geeignet. So wird eine Flexibilität erreicht, die später ein Erweitern oder Verkleinern einzelner Räume ermöglicht. Ferner können auch die Möbel neu angeordnet und die Bereiche neu verteilt werden, ohne dass dafür grosse Umbauten erforderlich sind.

Transparent materials create a sensation of space and, when combined with circular designs, afford a contemporary feel to the place.

Los materiales transparentes dan la sensación de amplitud y, junto con diseños circulares, remiten hacia lo contemporáneo.

Les matériaux transparents agrandissent les pièces. Utilisés pour un design de forme circulaire, ils apportent une touche contemporaine à l'ensemble.

Durchsichtige Materialien erwecken den Eindruck von Weite und –zusammen mit runden Designs– wirken sie sehr modern.

Getting the temperature conditions right in the workplace is vital. Direct sunlight can be regulated by strategically positioning mullions on the front of the building. These components may be made of wood or metal, depending on the required visual effect, and provide partial or total shading for wall openings.

El confort climático es primordial en los espacios de trabajo. La radiación solar directa se puede regular colocando estratégicamente parteluces en las fachadas. Estas piezas, que pueden ser de madera o metal según convenga a la estética de la edificación, permiten sombrear los vanos total o parcialmente.

Une bonne température est essentielle dans un espace de travail. On peut, grâce à des brise-soleil bien placés sur les murs, atténuer les effets des rayons solaires directs. Les brise-soleil couvrent totalement ou partiellement les fenêtres pour apporter de l'ombre. En bois ou en métal, ils s'adapteront à l'esthétique générale.

Klimatischer Komfort ist sehr wichtig in Arbeitsbereichen. Direktes Sonnenlicht kann durch strategisch angebrachte Sonnenblenden an der Fassade reguliert werden. Diese können aus Holz oder Metall gefertigt sein, je nachdem, was der Ästhetik des Gebäudes eher zu Gute kommt. So können die Fenster ganz oder teilweise abgeschattet werden.

Visual cleanliness for offices is a feasible option today thanks to the widespread use of wireless and portable work tools that no longer require clumsy installations. False floors and soffits offer an ideal way to conceal more complex installations such as air conditioning, and electric and telephone cables.

Hoy es factible tener oficinas visualmente limpias gracias a que una buena parte de las herramientas de trabajo son inalámbricas, portátiles y no necesitan instalaciones estorbosas. Para ocultar las instalaciones más complejas –aires acondicionados, cableados eléctricos y telefónicos...– los pisos y plafones falsos son el recurso adecuado.

Il est facile aujourd'hui de donner à son bureau un aspect net et ordonné car une grande partie du matériel d'entreprise est sans fil et transportable. Les installations électriques sont donc réduites. Pour en parfaire l'esthétique, on peut également dissimuler les câbles d'alimentation indispensables (air conditionné, électricité, téléphonie) dans les sols ou les faux-plafonds.

Heute ist es möglich, die Büros visuell sauber zu halten, da eine Grosszahl der Arbeitsmittel schnurlos und tragbar sind und keine störenden Installationen benötigen. Um komplexere Installationen zu verbergen, wie zum Beispiel Klimaanlagen, Elektro- und Telefonkabel, wird auf abgehängte Decken und hohle Böden zurückgegriffen.

There are two excellent ways to design an area for meetings. One is the traditional meetings room equipped with the necessary technology and a long table around which the event is held. The other is a small area with comfortable lounge furniture set around a small table. Or you can use both options at once if there is enough room, but it is advisable to bear in mind that the decision depends on the type of meetings that will take place there. The first option will create a more formal setting while the second makes for a relaxed ambience.

Existen dos alternativas interesantes para diseñar espacios de reunión; una de ellas es la sala de juntas tradicional equipada tecnológicamente y amueblada con mesa larga en torno a la cual se interactúa; la otra es un área con una sala cómoda y mesita central. Si el espacio es suficiente incluso se puede tener ambas opciones, pero cuando hay que elegir es útil saber que la decisión depende del tipo de reuniones que se tengan. La primera posibilidad sirve para crear contextos más rígidos y la segunda funciona para generar ambientes más relajados.

Le design d'une salle de réunion peut revêtir deux formes. La première est traditionnelle avec un équipement technologique classique et une grande table autour de laquelle les intervenants s'expriment. La seconde prend les apparences d'une pièce confortable avec une petite table centrale. Si la salle est assez vaste, il est possible d'associer ces deux formes. S'il faut choisir, il faut toujours le faire en fonction du genre de réunions qui vont s'y dérouler. Une réunion formelle, devra avoir lieu dans le premier type de salles alors que la seconde favorisera les échanges plus informels.

Es gibt zwei interessante Alternativen für das Design von Sitzungsräumen. Eine ist der traditionelle Sitzungsraum, der mit Technologie ausgestattet ist und einen langen Tisch aufweist, der das Zentrum der Interaktion darstellt. Eine andere Alternative ist ein Bereich mit einem bequemen Raum und einem Tisch in der Mitte. Ist der Raum gross genug, können sogar beide Möglichkeiten verwirklicht werden. Muss aber zwischen ihnen entschieden werden, sollte sich nach der Art von Sitzungen gerichtet werden, die dort abgehalten werden sollen. Die erste Art von Versammlungsraum ist für förmlichere Sitzungen geeignet und die zweite Art schafft eine entspanntere Atmosphäre.

SETS OF VERTICAL PLANES (affording height) and horizontal planes (affording depth) provide visual freedom between one zone and another and encourage socialization. A good way to do this is to use transparent materials on handrails and panels. These dynamic designs are ideal for restaurants, bars and nightclubs, but it is essential to carefully examine the different levels they generate in terms of passageways, accessibility, service times and other factors.

restaurants
restaurantes

LOS JUEGOS DE PLANOS VERTICALES –alturas– y horizontales –profundidades– propician libertad visual entre una zona y otra, favoreciendo la socialización. Para mantener este atributo conviene usar materiales transparentes tanto en barandales como en cerramientos. Si bien estos disenos son dinámicos y acertados en restaurantes, bares y centros nocturnos, es muy importante estudiar los desniveles que se forman, en función de recorridos, circulaciones, tiempos de servicio, entre otros factores.

L'INTERACTIVITÉ entre surfaces verticales (les hauteurs) et horizontales (les profondeurs) stimule la liberté visuelle entre les espaces et favorise los échanges entre convives. Pour maintenir cette particularité, il est recommandé d'utiliser des matériaux transparents pour toutes les séparations comme des parapets ou des cloisons. Ce type de design dynamise l'endroit et convient parfaitement aux restaurants, bars et boîtes de nuit. Mais les différents niveaux du sol doivent aussi être pensés pour que les couloirs, les lieux de passage et le temps que nécessite chaque service offert aux clients, par exemple, restent acceptables.

VERTIKALE EBENEN –Höhen– und horizontale Ebenen –Tiefen– führen zu einer visuellen Freiheit zwischen den Bereichen und fördern den Kontakt. Soll dieses Attribut erhalten bleiben, sind transparente Materialien geeignet, sowohl für Geländer als auch für Wände. Diese Designs sind sehr dynamisch und angebracht für Restaurants, Bars und Nachtclubs, dennoch sollten aber unbedingt die unterschiedlichen Ebenen analysiert werden, damit der Durchlauf, die Bedienzeiten usw. nicht beeinträchtigt werden.

One of the main objectives of restaurant design is to create
a pleasant, comfortable and suggestive setting. A decorative
scheme based on paler tones of lilac, violet and purple will
give the space a distinct sheen given that these colors are
good at catching light. It also combines spectacularly with
orange-colored translucent hanging lamps and sparkling
effects at different points in the room.

Crear un entorno agradable, cómodo y sugerente es uno
de los primeros objetivos de un restaurante. La decoración
en lilas, violetas y púrpuras en sus gamas claras aporta
un brillo particular al espacio, pues son colores que al ser
iluminados atrapan la luz. Esta selección se alía de maravilla
con lámparas colgantes translúcidas en tonos naranjas y la
inclusión de destellos salpicados en el espacio.

Une atmosphère évocatrice, agréable et confortable est le
premier objectif de tout restaurant. Une décoration à base de lilas,
violet et pourpre clairs apporte un éclat particulier à l'endroit car
ces couleurs, sous l'effet des luminaires, captent la lumière. Des
lampes suspendues translucides de teinte orangée projetant des
fragments lumineux conviendront parfaitement à cette décoration.

In einem Restaurant soll vor allem eine angenehme, bequeme
und anregende Umgebung geschaffen werden. Eine Dekoration in
hellem lila, violett und purpur verleiht dem Raum einen besonderen
Glanz, denn es handelt sich um Farben, die bei Beleuchtung das
Licht einfangen. Diese Wahl kombiniert vortrefflich mit Hängelampen
in Orangetönen, sowie im Raum verteiltem Glitzern.

The intended ambience is what will determine the best options for coverings, coatings, upholstery, shapes, colors, textures, furniture style and decorative items. Upholstery and table linen textures that are soft to the touch generate a feeling of hospitality, as do armchairs with rounded backrests, warm-toned lighting and a fireplace. Coverings and coatings such as wood generate a cozy atmosphere, while spatial forms with an extended apex afford a more dynamic feel to the place. These effects can be enhanced if they are repeated on soffits and floors.

En un restaurante o en un bar la selección de recubrimientos, tapicerías, formas espaciales, colores, texturas, estilo de mobiliario y elementos de ornato depende mucho del ambiente que se intente conseguir. Las texturas suaves al tacto en tapicería y mantelería provocan sensación de hospitalidad, igual que los sillones con respaldos curvos, las luces en tonos cálidos o el fuego de una chimenea. El uso de recubrimientos como la madera detonan un clima acogedor y las formas espaciales con vértices prolongados evocan dinamismo, efectos que se subrayan si se les repite en plafones y pesos.

Dans un restaurant ou un bar, le choix des matériaux, des tapis, des formes particulières, des couleurs, des textures, du style de meubles et des ornementations dépend beaucoup de l'atmosphère que l'on veut créer. Les tapis ou le linge de table doux au toucher donnent la sensation de se trouver dans un lieu accueillant. C'est aussi le cas des fauteuils à dossier arrondis, la lumière chaude ou le feu d'une cheminée. Un matériau comme le bois contribue à faire de l'endroit un espace confortable et les formes élancées dynamisent les lieux, en particulier au plafond et au sol.

In einem Restaurant oder einer Bar hängt die Auswahl von Beschichtungen, Stoffen, Raumform, Farben, Texturen, Möbelstil und Dekoration von der Atmosphäre ab, die erzielt werden soll. Weiche Texturen für Bezugstoffe und Tischdecken erwecken den Eindruck von Gastlichkeit, genau wie Sessel mit gebogenen Lehnen, warme Lichtfarbtöne oder das Feuer in einem offenen Kamin. Beschichtungen wie Holz, erzeugen eine gemütliche Atmosphäre und Raumformen mit langen Scheitelpunkten wirken dynamisch. Diese Effekte werden noch verstärkt, wenn sie auf abgehängten Decken und Böden wiederholt werden.

Large windows are the best way to make the most of a spectacular view.

Abrir las vistas con extensos ventanales vidriados es la solución de diseño más adecuada si se cuenta con un paisaje espectacular.

Un design axé sur la vue extérieure avec de grandes vitres est on ne peut plus adéquat lorsque l'on peut profiter d'un paysage exceptionnel.

Wenn eine spektakuläre Landschaft vorhanden ist, sind grosse Fensterscheiben die geeignetste Designlösung.

Some structural and architectural components can be both functional and esthetic at the same time. Wood is a good option for this dual role, and can be used to line columns or in an attractive partitioning wall based on simple panels.

Hay elementos estructurales y arquitectónicos que pueden ser funcionales y decorativos a la vez. La madera es un material muy noble para estos fines; se puede usar tanto como revestimiento de columnas como para formar un atractivo muro divisorio basado en simples tablillas.

Certains éléments structurels et architecturaux sont aussi bien fonctionnels que décoratifs. Le bois est un matériau qui correspond bien à ce genre de définition puisqu'il est possible de l'utiliser pour recouvrir des colonnes et pour créer un mur de séparation à l'esthétique recherchée avec de simples lattes.

Es gibt strukturelle und architektonische Elemente, die gleichzeitig funktionell und dekorativ sind. Holz ist ein sehr edles Material, das zu diesem Zweck eingesetzt werden kann. Es kann zur Verkleidung von Säulen und für eine attraktive Trennwand verwendet werden, die aus einfachen Tafeln besteht.

stores
tiendas
boutiques
geschäfte

WHEN IT COMES TO COMMERCIAL PREMISES, the competition to entice consumers is now fiercer than ever and is prompting designers to be more creative than before. With a little originality and resourcefulness, certain architectural and/or decorative elements can be transformed into the main feature of a given space. The wall of a boutique, for instance, can act like a backdrop whose texture and color bring out the qualities of the garments on sale.

EN EL ÁMBITO DE LOS ESPACIOS COMERCIALES la competencia por seducir al consumidor es cada vez mayor y propicia la creatividad de los diseñadores. Existen elementos arquitectónicos y/o decorativos a los que, con cierta originalidad e inventiva, se les puede convertir en protagonistas del espacio. Por ejemplo, el muro de una tienda de ropa que, como si fuera un telón de fondo, exalta con su textura y color las cualidades de las prendas.

DANS L'UNIVERS DES GALERIES MARCHANDES, la concurrence, toujours plus grande pour séduire les consommateurs, stimule les créateurs en matière de design. Avec un peu d'originalité et d'invention on peut transformer certains éléments architecturaux ou décoratifs (ou les deux) en pièces maîtresse de la décoration de l'endroit. Un exemple : ce mur d'une boutique de vêtements, qui, telle une toile de fond, fait ressortir les qualités des produits grâce à sa texture et à sa couleur.

IM BEREICH VON GESCHÄFTEN wird die Konkurrenz in Bezug auf die Verführung der Konsumenten immer grösser und fordert die Kreativität der Designer heraus. Es gibt architektonische und/oder dekorative Elemente, die sich auf originelle und erfinderische Weise in die Hauptdarsteller des Bereiches verwandeln. Zum Beispiel die Wand eines Bekleidungsgeschäftes, die durch ihre Textur und Farbe die Qualitäten der Kleidung hervorhebt, als ob es sich um einen Stoff im Hintergrund handeln würde.

Decoration in stores must benefit the products and never compete with them. This can be done in simple and neutral settings where the gleam and sparkling effects of the lighting provide the spatial accents, while the true stars of the show are the items on sale. These products are given an even more prominent role by the right-angled furnishings and the peripheral location of the shelves to create isles for display and/or directing attention to the center of the store.

La decoración de establecimientos comerciales debe encauzarse a beneficiar al producto y nunca a competir con él, lo cual es más fácil garantizar a través de ambientes sobrios y neutros, donde los acentos espaciales recaen en los brillos y destellos de la iluminación y las estrellas del espectáculo son los propios artículos.
Las formas del mobiliario basadas en ángulos rectos así como la ubicación perimetral de los anaqueles, dejando islas de exhibición y/o apoyo al centro, son aspectos que favorecen también el lucimiento de los productos.

La décoration des établissements commerciaux doit toujours promouvoir les produits que l'on y vend et non les concurrencer. Pour ne pas oublier ce postulat, on optera pour des atmosphères sobres et neutres, avec une décoration reposant sur une lumière dont les multiples reflets étincelants mettent en valeur les vrais protagonistes de l'endroit que sont les articles en vente. Un mobilier caractérisé par des angles droits et des étagères autour des pièces pour laisser la place au centre à des espaces ou des stands promotionnels sont également souhaitables pour mettre en valeur les produits.

Die Dekoration in Geschäften muss darauf ausgerichtet sein, die Produkte vorteilhaft darzustellen, wobei niemals mit ihnen konkurriert werden darf. Dies kann durch nüchterne und neutrale Atmosphären sichergestellt werden, bei denen die Akzente im Raum lediglich der Glanz und das Glitzern der Beleuchtung sind. Die Stars im Mittelpunkt sind einzig und allein die Artikel selbst. Möbel mit rechten Winkeln und eine perimetrale Anordnung der Regale mit Ausstellungs- und Hilfsinseln in der Mitte sind Aspekte, die die Darstellung der Produkte zusätzlich begünstigen.

A glass façade is a seductive way to separate public areas from semi-public ones, thanks to the sensation of continuity between indoors and outdoors generated by its transparency. This makes things interesting for people walking past on the street and for anyone inside the place. The ideal complement for this kind of ambience is a majestic curved staircase with light passing freely between the different steps, as it takes this interplay of light indoors and increases visibility.

Una fachada de vidrio es una solución seductora para separar espacios públicos y semi-públicos, pues su transparencia produce la sensación de continuidad entre interior y exterior; de este modo, lo que sucede es interesante tanto para el que circula por afuera como para quien está adentro. Una magestuosa escalera curva que deje que la luz pase libremente entre un escalón y otro es el complemento perfecto para este tipo de diseños, pues permite que el juego luminoso se extienda también hacia el interior, además de facilitar la visibilidad.

e verre est une solution attrayante pour séparer des lieux publics des endroits semi-publics car la transparence ne sépare pas complètement l'intérieur de l'extérieur. Tout ce qui se passe dans le magasin est intéressant pour quelqu'un à l'intérieur comme pour une personne dehors. Un magnifique escalier en colimaçon, dont les marches laissent librement passer la lumière, est le complément parfait pour ce type de design, le magasin profitant de la clarté avec une visibilité améliorée.

ine Glasfassade ist eine verführerische Lösung, um öffentliche Bereiche von halb-öffentlichen Bereichen abzutrennen, denn die Transparenz erweckt den Eindruck von Kontinuität zwischen den Innen- und Aussenbereichen. Auf diese Weise ist das Geschehen sowohl von aussen interessant anzusehen, als auch für diejenigen, die sich im Inneren befinden. Eine majestätische, urvige Treppe, die das Licht frei zwischen den Stufen hindurchscheinen lässt, ist die perfekte Ergänzung für diese Art von Design. s wird ermöglicht, dass das Lichterspiel auch im Inneren fortgesetzt wird und erleichtert gleichzeitig die Sichtbarkeit.

miscellaneous spaces
espacios diversos
lieux divers
verschiedene bereiche

shopping malls
centros comerciales
centres commerciaux
einkaufszentren

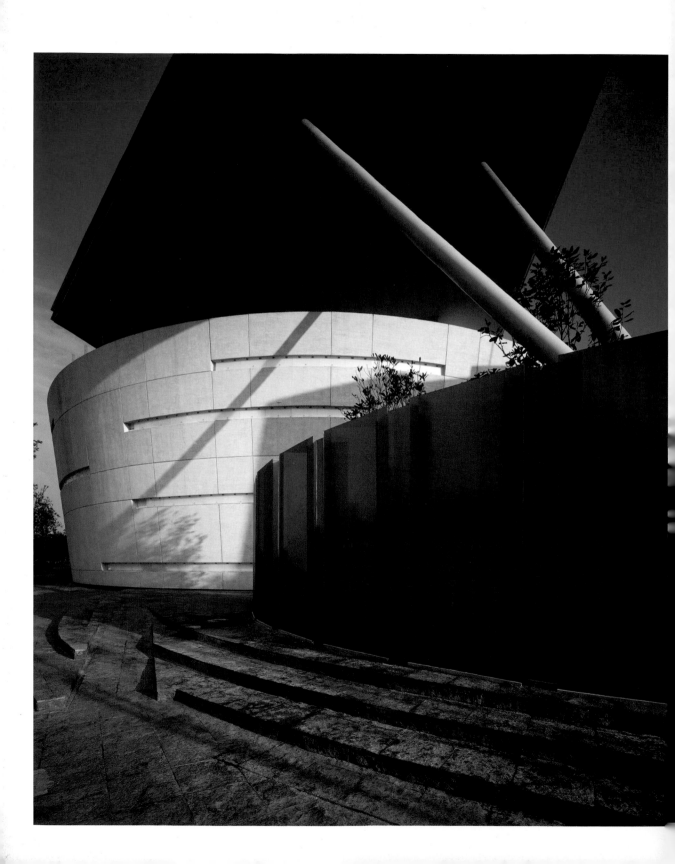

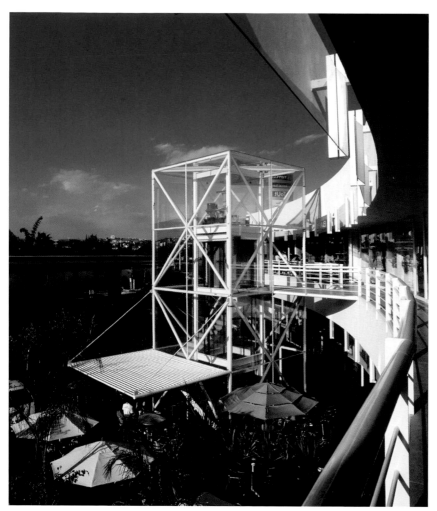

For large spaces without a ceiling, the best bet is to create a number of darker and sheltered spots using a range of different options. One possibility is a lattice window or a flat structure with a lattice roof; or you could install a roof garden or columns holding up lengthwise and cross-sectional beams. An absolute must is tensile structures with textile covers, preferably waterproof to provide protection from the rain as well as the sun. The traditional sunshades over tables placed in different locations are equally useful.

En espacios de gran escala y sin techumbre lo más aconsejable es crear diversas zonas sombrías y de protección, combinando distintas alternativas. Alguna de ellas puede ser una celosía o cualquier estructura plana con techo enrejado; también es factible incluir una pérgola o columnas que soporten vigas longitudinales y transversales; desde luego, no pueden faltar las tenso estructuras con cubiertas textiles, de preferencia impermeables para proteger no sólo del sol sino también de la lluvia. Las tradicionales sombrillas en mesas son igualmente útiles si se colocan en distintos lados.

Pour des lieux très vastes qui ne sont pas couverts, il est recommandé de créer des zones d'ombres et protégées en adoptant plusieurs solutions. L'une d'elles peut être constituée par un toit avec jalousies ou toute autre surface plane comprenant des ouvertures. On peut aussi opter pour une pergola ou des colonnes supportant des poutres longitudinales et transversales. Les toitures avec des toiles tendues, si possible imperméables pour protéger du soleil et de la pluie, sont bien évidemment envisageables. Enfin, les parasols aux tables des terrasses sont également utiles si on les place à différents endroits.

In grossen Räumen ohne Dach, ist es angebracht verschiedene Schattenbereiche zu schaffen, die Schutz bieten. Es können dazu verschiedene Alternativen zur Anwendung kommen. So können zum Beispiel Streben oder eine flache Konstruktion mit gitterförmigem Dach verwendet werden. Eine andere Möglichkeit ist der Einbezug von Laubengängen oder Säulen, die längs- und querstehende Balken tragen. Ausserdem sollten natürlich gespannte Strukturen aus Textilabdeckungen nicht fehlen, vorzugsweise aus wetterfestem Material, um nicht nur vor Sonne, sondern auch vor Regen zu schützen. Traditionelle Sonnenschirme über den Tischen sind genauso nützlich, wenn sie an unterschiedlichen Stellen angebracht werden.

Steel is used in shopping malls for both structural and ornamental purposes. Stainless steel is especially suitable for outdoor furniture, pot plants, signs and handrails, thanks to the use of chrome and other metals to make it rust-proof.

El acero en la construcción de centros comerciales es empleado como material estructural y con fines decorativos. El acero inoxidable es particularmente adecuado para espacios exteriores en mobiliario, macetas, señalización, barandales... pues, debido a que contiene cromo y otros metales, es resistente a la corrosión.

L'acier est un matériau structurel et décoratif employé dans la construction des centres commerciaux. L'acier inoxydable est particulièrement indiqué pour l'extérieur comme pour le mobilier toujours dehors, les pots de fleurs, les panneaux de signalisation, les rampes d'escalier ..., car il contient du chrome et d'autres métaux qui résistent à la corrosion.

Stahl wird beim Bau von Einkaufszentren als strukturelles Material verwendet, das auch dekorative Zwecke erfüllt. Rostfreier Edelstahl ist beonders für Möbel, Blumentöpfe, Schilder und Geländer in den Aussenbereichen geeignet, denn da es Chrom und andere Metalle enthält, rostet es nicht.

apartments
apartamentos
appartements
wohnungen

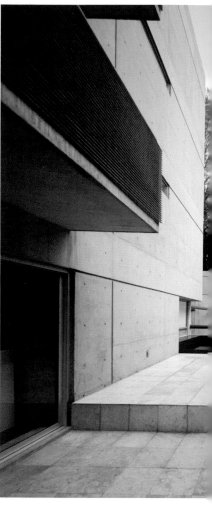

Volume is an eloquent expression of shape, which means the more interesting the combination of the latter is, the more striking the former will be. A space can be projected in many ways. The use of blocks based on pure and simple shapes can create a tranquil effect, while differently-shaped architectural components and volumes generate a sense of flow. Shape and volume can be reinforced by contrasting materials or accentuating their outlines through the use of light. The shadows cast by volumes and cast on them during the day also play an important role in the overall result.

Dado que el volumen es la expresión de las formas, cuanto más interesante es la combinación de éstas, tanto más excepcional resulta aquél. Existen muchas maneras de proyectar el espacio; a veces con bloques de formas puras y simples se alcanza una estética serena; otras con cuerpos y elementos arquitectónicos de formas diversas se consigue el movimiento;... Formas y volúmenes se refuerzan contrastando materiales o perfilando sus siluetas con luz. Son también parte de la composición las sombras que crean los volúmenes y las que se posan sobre ellos durante el día.

Le volume est l'expression des formes. Plus la composition des formes est recherchée et plus le volume sera exceptionnel. On peut mettre en valeur l'espace de plusieurs façons. Par exemple, une esthétique caractérisée par une certaine sérénité peut être créée avec des éléments architecturaux de formes pures et simples. En revanche, une esthétique dynamique comporte des éléments de formes variées. Les effets produits par les formes et les volumes seront renforcés si l'on joue sur les contrastes entre les matériaux et si l'on affine leurs contours en utilisant la lumière. L'ombre est également utile pour créer des volumes ou pour en modifier l'aspect pendant la journée.

Das Aussehen hängt vom Ausdruck der Formen ab, und je interessanter sie kombiniert wurden, desto ausserordentlicher ist das Ergebnis. Es gibt viele Möglichkeiten zur Gestaltung eines Bereiches. Es können Blocks mit klaren und einfachen Formen verwendet werden, die dann den Eindruck von Ruhe hervorrufen. Durch Verwendung von architektonischen Körpern und Elementen, die unterschiedliche Formen aufweisen, wird Bewegung erzielt. Formen und Ebenen werden noch verstärkt, wenn verschiedenartige Materialien zum Einsatz kommen oder ihr Umriss beleuchtet wird. Auch einen Teil des Designs bilden die Schatten, die durch die Ebenen entstehen und sich im Verlauf des Tages verändern.

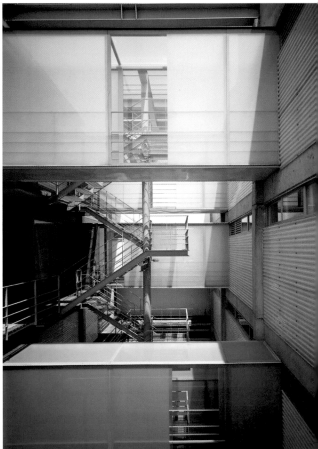

The use of steel grating was once the exclusive terrain of industry, but for over a decade now it has featured as architectural tools in the form of lattice windows, soffits, terraces, handrails, window protectors and even floors. One of its benefits is that it creates open areas through which plenty of light, air and heat can circulate.

El uso de las rejillas de acero se limitaba a la industria, pero desde hace más de una década éstas se utilizan en arquitectura como celosías, plafones, terrazas, barandales, protectores de ventanas y pisos. Entre sus ventajas están el conformar áreas abiertas que dejan pasar luz, aire y calor de un espacio al otro.

Les grilles en acier étaient auparavant utilisés simplement dans l'industrie. Mais depuis plus de dix ans, elles sont employées en architecture pour des jalousies, des toitures, des terrasses, des parapets et pour protéger les fenêtres ou les sols. L'avantage principal des grilles réside dans le fait qu'elles créent des espaces ouverts en laissant passer la lumière, l'air et la chaleur entre deux pièces.

Der Gebrauch von Stahlgittern war der Industrie vorbehalten, aber seit mehr als einem Jahrzehnt werden sie auch in der Architektur als Fenstergitter, abgehängte Decken, Terrassen, Geländer und Schutz von Fenstern und Böden verwendet. Ihre Vorteile sind, dass sie in offenen Bereichen das Licht, die Luft und die Wärme von einem Ort an den anderen hindurchlassen.

Common areas like lobbies, receptions, swimming pools and terraces must be comfortable and conducive to free movement.

Las áreas de uso común como lobbies, recepciones, piscinas o terrazas deben ser cómodas y con circulaciones fluidas.

Les espaces collectifs comme les halls, les salles de réception, les piscines ou les terrasses doivent être conçus pour être confortable et pour qu'on puisse s'y déplacer sans problème.

Bereiche wie Lobbys, Rezeptionen, Schwimmbäder und Terrassen sollten bequem sein und den Durchgangsverkehr erleichtern.

The balanced outdoor interplay between steel grating and large windows and openings highlights the formal look of volumes and suggests lightness." The greenery of nature is a crucial presence that offsets the coldness of glass and steel. The translucent qualities of glass and the visibility afforded by the gratings in different parts of the construction allow flow between the inside and outside of the building, while wood and stone floors are evocative of nature.

En exteriores, el juego equilibrado de rejillas de acero y grandes áreas de ventanas y oquedades hace que se destaque el aspecto formal de los volúmenes y sugiere ligereza. La inclusión del verde de la naturaleza es indispensable para compensar la frialdad del vidrio y el acero. La translucidez del vidrio y la visibilidad que permiten las rejillas usadas en distintas partes del edificio crean la sensación de comunicación entre interior y exterior, en tanto que los pisos de madera y piedra vuelven a remitir a la naturaleza.

Si l'on veut mettre en valeur la simplicité et la légéreté des volumes extérieurs, il est recommandé de jouer sur l'équilibre entre les grilles en acier et les fenêtres et autres ouvertures. Ici, le vert, couleur de la nature, est indispensable pour atténuer la froideur associée aux vitres et à l'acier. De même, le fait que le verre soit translucide et que les grilles favorisent la visibilité donnent l'impression qu'il n'y a pas vraiment de séparation entre l'intérieur et l'extérieur. Quant aux sols en bois et en pierre, ils nous font de nouveau penser à la nature.

Im Aussenbereich führt eine ausgewogene Kombination von Stahlgittern mit grossen Fenstern und Öffnungen dazu, dass der formelle Aspekt hervorgehoben wird, wobei gleichzeitig eine Leichtigkeit angedeutet wird. Der Einbezug des Grün der Natur ist unabdingbar zum Ausgleich der Kälte von Glas und Stahl. Die Durchsichtigkeit des Glases und die Sichtbarkeit, die durch die Gitter erzielt wird, die an verschiedenen Stellen des Gebäudes angebracht wurden, führen zu einem Eindruck von Kommunikation zwischen dem Innen- und Aussenbereich, da die Holz- und Steinböden wieder das Thema Natur aufnehmen.

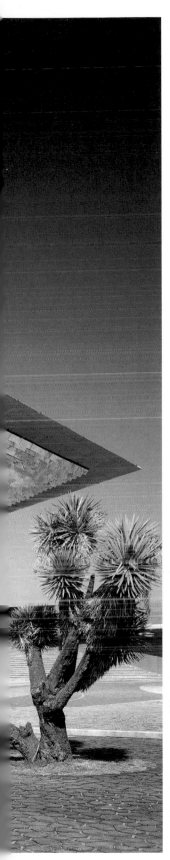

The main areas in an auditorium –esplanade, entrance, ticket office– need to bear some degree of relevance and visibility with each other, as well as with the inside and the surroundings. This can be achieved using split levels, stairs, vantage points and peripheral passageways if the design is very plastic and in synch with the scales.

En un auditorio los espacios exteriores principales –explanada, acceso, taquillas– deben guardar relación y visibilidad entre sí, además de con el interior y el entorno. Desniveles, escalinatas, miradores y circulaciones perimetrales son opciones con las que se llega a esta meta cuando el diseño es muy plástico y está acorde con las escalas.

Pour un auditorium, les principaux espaces extérieurs comme l'esplanade, les chemins d'accès ou la zone des guichets doivent maintenir une certaine relation visuelle entre eux comme avec l'intérieur et ce qu'on trouve à proximité du bâtiment. A l'extérieur, on peut prévoir différents niveaux, des escaliers, des endroits conçus pour profiter de la vue et des chemins périphériques lorsque l'on opte pour un design très souple à l'échelle du bâtiment.

In einem Auditorium müssen die hauptsächlichen Aussenbereiche, wie Esplanade, Zugang und Schalter, zueinander passen und Sichtbarkeit aufweisen, was auch für den Innenbereich und die Umgebung gilt. Verschiedenen Ebenen, Treppen, Aussichtspunkte und perimetrale Durchgänge sind hierzu geeinet, sofern es sich um ein sehr plastisches Design handelt, das auch vom Maßstab her passt.

One attractive solution for the outside of a building is to extend the roof a few meters beyond the rest of the construction, like an architectural mortarboard. One side of the extension can be used to house something that will really catch the public's eye, such as placing mirror glass mullions under the extension to reflect a work of art and create a highly original mural in a very unexpected location. Stairs and ramps can offer an excellent vantage point on this extraordinary creation.

Una solución atrayente al exterior de un edificio público es volar varios metros su cubierta, como si ésta fuera un "birrete" de la construcción. Es factible aprovechar algún extremo del volado para desarrollar una imagen de interés para el público. Una posibilidad es ubicar estratégicamente bajo el volado parteluces de cristal espejo para reflejar una obra de arte, generando un mural muy original y colocado en un sitio no acostumbrado. Las escaleras o las rampas pueden funcionar como miradores de esta sorprendente pieza.

Une option esthétique pour l'aspect extérieur d'un bâtiment public consiste à le surmonter d'une toiture qui dépasse de quelques mètres ses dimensions, comme si le toit le « chapeautait » en quelques sortes. Et on l'on peut utiliser les quelques mètres en plus pour personnaliser l'édifice avec, par exemple, des brise-soleil sous la forme de miroir qui reflèteront une œuvre d'art afin de créer une façade très originale dans un endroit inhabituel. Avec un édifice aussi exceptionnel, les escaliers et les rampes d'accès peuvent également être des endroits où l'on profitera de la vue.

Eine reizvolle Lösung im Aussenbereich eines öffentlichen Gebäudes ist ein Vorsprung von einigen Metern, als ob es sich um ein „Barett" des Baus handele. An der Spitze des Vorsprunges kann dann etwas angebracht werden, das das Interesse des Publikums erweckt. Eine Möglichkeit ist das strategische Anbringen von Mittelsäulen aus Spiegelglas, um ein Kunstwerk widerzuspiegeln. So entsteht ein sehr originelles Wandbild, das sich an einem sehr ungewöhnlichen Ort befindet. Die Treppen oder Rampen können die Funktion eines Aussichtspunktes zur Besichtigung dieses überraschenden Stückes übernehmen.

hotels   hoteles   hôtels

The architecture of the mid-Twentieth century can be combined with the contemporary style to generate a pleasant indoor contrast between old and new, as well as strengthen the esthetic concept by following the style of the façades.

Combinar la arquitectura de principios del siglo XX con el diseño arquitectónico contemporáneo es un recurso que, además de beneficiar al contexto al respetar los rasgos estilísticos de las fachadas, forja en el interior un agradable contraste entre lo nuevo y lo viejo.

Associer l'architecture du début du XXe siècle avec un design architectural contemporain est une solution qui, tout en respectant le style des façades, permet un intéressant contraste entre ancien et nouveau à l'intérieur.

Die Kombination der Architektur des frühen XX. Jahrhunderts mit moderner Architektur ist eine Lösung, die die stilistischen Züge der Fassaden hervorhebt und im Inneren einen angenehmen Kontrast zwischen alt und neu schafft.

When it comes to deciding which color and texture to use on large surfaces, it is important to consider the presence, intensity and tone of light.

En la decisión de color y textura de grandes superficies es fundamental considerar la presencia de la luz, su intensidad y tono.

Lorsque l'on choisit la couleur et la texture d'un matériau pour une grande surface, il est fondamental de ne pas oublier les effets de la lumière, son intensité et sa tonalité.

Bei der Wahl von Farbe und Textur von grossen Oberflächen ist es wichtig, das Vorhandensein von Licht, sowie dessen Intensität und Farbton zu berücksichtigen.

An avant-garde look can be created with an interplay of planes based on alternating opaque and transparent materials and using textures and colors at different depths. If you use this type of combination, however, it is advisable not to employ any further decorative options.

Los juegos de planos alternando materiales opacos y transparentes y haciendo convivir textura y color a distintas profundidades constituyen una propuesta vanguardista. No obstante, es recomendable no realizar más acciones decorativas cuando se eligen estas combinaciones.

Les jeux entre surfaces planes où l'on contraste des matériaux opaques et transparents ainsi que des textures et des couleurs différentes pour des espaces plus ou moins profonds sont considérés comme avant-gardistes. Toutefois, il est recommandé de ne pas surcharger cette décoration avec d'autres associations esthétiques.

Die Kombination von Ebenen, die abwechselnd aus matten und durchsichtigen Materialien gefertigt sind, mit Texturen und Farben verschiedener Tiefe, führen zu einer avantgardistischen Lösung. Dennoch ist es empfehlenswert, bei Wahl dieser Kombination keine weiteren dekorativen Elemente zu verwenden.

A hotel lobby is much more than just a simple reception area for routing people towards the elevators. It is the place where guests and visitors are welcomed. The contemporary style requires simple, functional decoration, and one of its defining features is its emphasis on large and well-lit spaces. The walls are brightly-colored, while right angles, defined shapes and beige or brown upholstery distinguish the furniture. The details are generally discrete and the few items used are afforded a lead role.

El lobby de un hotel no es un simple recibidor que sirva de transición para redireccionar a la gente hacia los elevadores, es también el sitio para dar la bienvenida a huéspedes y visitantes. Si se opta por el estilo contemporáneo, la decoración es simple, funcional y se caracteriza por promover espacios amplios y luminosos. Los colores de los muros son claros y en el mobiliario dominan líneas rectas, formas definidas y lápices beiges y cafés. En general los detalles son discretos y, aunque hay pocos objetos, éstos son importantes.

La réception d'un hôtel n'est pas un simple lieu où l'on redirige les gens vers les ascenseurs. C'est aussi un endroit où l'on souhaite la bienvenue aux clients et aux visiteurs. Si l'on choisit le style contemporain pour la réception, la décoration sera simple et fonctionnelle avec d'amples espaces lumineux. Les murs seront de couleur claire et les lignes droites avec des formes définies caractériseront le mobilier auquel on ajoutera des tapis beiges ou marron. Les détails, en général, resteront discrets et les objets décoratifs, peu nombreux, n'en seront pas moins importants.

Die Lobby eines Hotels ist nicht nur eine einfache Empfangshalle, die zum Durchgang und zur Weiterleitung der Personen zu den Aufzügen dient. Es ist auch ein Ort, an dem die Gäste und Besucher willkommen geheissen werden. Wird ein moderner Stil gewählt, sollte die Dekoration einfach und funktionell sein, sowie grosse und hell erleuchtete Räume aufweisen. Die Farben der Wände sind hell und die Möbel haben gerade Linien, definierte Formen und Stoffe in beige oder braun. Im Allgemeinen sind die Details dezent und es sind nur wenige Objekte vorhanden, die aber sehr wichtig sind.

labs laboratorios laboratoires laboratorien

The architecture of labs is expected to project a sense of order, precision and cleanliness. The prefabricated panels used to cover the outside walls are visually perfect, as well as easy to clean and put in place.

Se espera que la arquitectura de un laboratorio transmita la imagen de orden, precisión y pulcritud. Los paneles prefabricados para revestir fachadas lucen perfectos a la vista, son de fácil limpieza y de rápida y sencilla colocación.

L'architecture d'un laboratoire doit, en général, nous donner l'impression de l'ordre, de la précision et de l'extrême propreté. Pour y parvenir, on peut utiliser divers matériaux, sous la forme de panneaux, pour décorer la façade. Très agréables pour l'œil, ces panneaux sont de plus rapides et faciles à poser.

Von der Architektur eines Labors wird erwartet, dass sie den Eindruck von Ordnung, Präzision und Reinheit erweckt. Vorgefertigte Paneele zur Verkleidung der Fassade sehen perfekt aus, sind leicht zu reinigen und können schnell und einfach angebracht werden.

Inside, the floors and walls lined with beech or some other light-colored wood stand out when cold, dim colors such as mint green or lavender-blue are used for other elements including the light. These settings can be complemented with polished or acid-treated glass, white furnishings and polished metal trims.

Los pisos y muros de haya o de cualquier madera clara resaltan cuando en el resto de los elementos, incluyendo la luz, se usan colores fríos y tenues como el verde menta y el azul lavanda. Estos ambientes se complementan con vidrios esmerilados o trabajados al ácido, mobiliario blanco y molduras de metales pulidos.

La couleur des sols et des murs en hêtre (ou dans un autre
bois clair) ressort lorsque les autres éléments décoratifs
(lumière comprise) sont de teintes froides et légères comme
le vert menthe et le lavande. Cette décoration peut être
complétée par des vitres en verre dépoli ou traité à l'acide,
par un mobilier blanc et par des moulures en métal poli.

Böden und Wände aus Buche oder einem anderen
hellen Holztyp werden hervorgehoben, wenn die
restlichen Elemente –das Licht mit inbegriffen- mit kalten
und blassen Farben ausgestattet werden, wie Mintgrün
und Lavendelblau. Diese Atmosphären werden durch
geschliffenes Glas oder Säurearbeiten, weisse Möbel und
Rahmen aus poliertem Metall vervollständigt.

A neutral atmosphere is the best way to bring out the full splendor of any museum exhibit, which is why it is essential for the architectural and decorative components not to compete with the objects on display. For visually appealing items, such as ironworks and fastening systems, the emphasis should be on their role more than their look.

A través de una atmósfera muy neutra se privilegia el lucimiento de cualquier exposición; por ello, conviene que ni los elementos arquitectónicos ni los decorativos compitan con los objetos de la muestra. Piezas llamativas como herrajes y sistemas de sujeción deben privilegiar su funcionalidad por encima de cualquier propósito decorativo.

Pour que l'endroit se caractérise par une atmosphère très neutre, il convient d'éclairer chaque objet exposé. Les éléments architecturaux ou décoratifs ne doivent donc pas être plus importants que les pièces présentées et les dispositifs voyants utilisés pour les exposer, comme tout ce qui relève des ferrures, doivent être avant tout fonctionnels, leur esthétique passant au second plan.

Ausstellungen kommen besonders zur Geltung, wenn sie in einer neutralen Atmospäre dargeboten werden. Daher sollten weder die architektonischen noch die dekorativen Elemente mit den ausgestellten Stücken konkurrieren. Auffällige Stücke, wie Beschläge und Befestigungssysteme sollten vor allem ihre Funktion erfüllen und weniger dekorativ sein.

Trabajo y lucha sindical

museums museos musées museen

One excellent option for a trip around a museum is to install other exhibitions on the ramps. If the ramps have the right slope and are made using non-slip materials they will assist the movement of visitors through the museum.

Una buena solución para resolver recorridos museísticos y otras exhibiciones son las rampas. Si éstas cuentan con la pendiente adecuada y están construidas con materiales antiderrapantes funcionan para que circule todo tipo de público.

Une bonne solution pour résoudre le problème posé par les zones de passage dans les musées ou dans tout autre lieu d'exposition consiste à placer plusieurs rampes d'accès. Correctement inclinées et comportant des matériaux antidérapants, le public dans son ensemble se déplacera sans difficulté.

Eine gute Lösung für Museumsflure und andere Ausstellungen sind Rampen. Wenn diese eine geeignete Neigung aufweisen und mit rutschfesten Materialien gefertigt wurden, so kann dort jede Art von Publikum verkehren.

architectonic arquitectónicos architectoniques architektonische

46-47 *architectural and interior design project:* ABAX, fernando de haro, jesús fernández, omar fuentes y bertha figueroa, *contributor:* javier espinosa

48-49 *architectural project:* ARQUITECH, juan josé sánchez-aedo y andrés santos

50-51 *architectural project:* ABAX, fernando de haro, jesús fernández, omar fuentes y bertha figueroa

52-53 *architectural project:* JSª, javier sánchez, *contributors:* jorge ambrosi, carlos malagnon, juan carral, mario nájera, julián barnabe, giovanni f. oteiza y patricia aceves

54-55 *architectural project:* ARQUITECH, juan josé sánchez-aedo y alejandro elizondo, *contributor:* miguel ángel garcía

56-57 *architectural project:* SO STUDIO, sergio orduña chapoy, *developers:* GRUPO CANBEC

58-59 *architectural project:* ARQUITECH, juan josé sánchez-aedo

60-61 *interior design:* ART ARQUITECTOS, antonio rueda ventosa, *architectural project:* CINEMEX

62-63 *architectural and interior design project:* FORMA ARQUITECTOS, eduardo ávalos, miguel de llano y josé segués

64-65 *interior design:* ART ARQUITECTOS, antonio rueda ventosa, *architectural project:* CINEMEX

66 a 69 *architectural project:* GRUPO CERO y ROCKWELL GROUP, *construction:* GRUPO CERO

70 *architectural project:* PASCAL ARQUITECTOS

71 (top and center) *architectural project:* PASCAL ARQUITECTOS, (bottom) *architectural project:* MARTOR ARQUITECTOS, enrique martorell y juan ricardo torres-landa, *contributors:* alejandro de noriega, mariana rodríguez, enrique melchor ruan, fernando carbajal pruneda y gerardo chacón reséndiz

72-73 *architectural project:* PASCAL ARQUITECTOS

74-75 *architectural project:* MARTOR ARQUITECTOS, enrique martorell y juan ricardo torres-landa, *contributors:* alejandro de noriega, mariana rodríguez, enrique melchor ruan y eliel zamora rangel

76-77 *architectural project:* ABAX, fernando de haro, jesús fernández, omar fuentes y bertha figueroa

78 a 81 *architectural project:* PASCAL ARQUITECTOS

82-83 *architectural project and construction:* HASBANI ARQUITECTOS, mayer hasbani, *contributors:* omar salas, josé luis ramírez y sofía cisneros otero, *structural design:* CAFEL INGENIERIA, PESA INGENIERIA, *soil mechanics:* gutiérrez cimentaciones, *hydrosanitary electrical installation:* instalaciones 2000, *air extraction:* CLIMA instalaciones

85 (top) *architectural project:* JSª, javier sánchez, paola calzada, mariana paz y diana elizalde, (bottom) *architectural project:* JSª, javier sánchez, paola calzada y larissa kadner

86 (top left and right) *architectural project:* JSª, javier sánchez, paola calzada, mariana paz y diana elizalde, (bottom) *architectural project:* JSª, javier sánchez, paola calzada y larissa kadner

87 *architectural project:* JSª, javier sánchez, paola calzada y larissa kadner

88-89 *architectural project:* oscar m. cadena, *contributor:* sandra fernández falcón, *estructural engineering:* jorge a. pérez, *electric engineering:* humberto gonzález y javier martínez, *water supply and sanitary engineering:* arturo morelos, *construction:* grupo constructor la seca

90 *architectural project:* B+P, alejandro bernardi gallo y beatriz peschard mijares y GA&A arquitectos, (center) *architectural and interior design project:* JSª, javier sánchez, paola calzada y mariana sánchez, (right) *architectural project:* SAMA ARQUITECTOS, rafael sama

90-91 *architectural project:* ABAX, fernando de haro, jesús fernández, omar fuentes y bertha figueroa

92 *architectural and interior design project:* GRUPO ARQUITECH, juan josé sánchez-aedo, *contributor:* alejandro viniegra, *construction:* ARQUITECH CONSTRUCTORA

94-95 *architectural project:* ARTECK, francisco guzmán-giraud

96-97 *architectural and interior design project:* SPACE, juan carlos baumgartner, *contributors:* loreto rodríguez blanco y francisco montoya

98-99 *architectural project:* SPACE, juan carlos baumgartner, *contributors:* gabriel téllez, karina díaz y francisco montoya, *lighting:* kai diederichsen, *contractor:* GA & A

100-101 *architectural project:* SPACE, juan carlos baumgartner, *contributors:* gabriel téllez, gabriel salazar y francisco montoya, *lighting:* kai diederichsen, *contractor:* alpha-hardin

102-103 *architectural project:* B+P, alejandro bernardi gallo y beatriz peschard mijares y GA&A arquitectos

104-105 *architectural project:* SPACE, juan carlos baumgartner

106-107 *interior design:* TORBELI, elena talavera, *architectural project:* carlos felipe salomón, *contributors:* alberto tello, martha lópez y carmen escutia

108 a 111 *architectural and interior design project:* JSª, javier sánchez, *contributor:* paola calzada y mariana sánchez,

112 a 115 *architectural project:* GRUPO CERO y ROCKWELL GROUP, *construction:* GRUPO CERO

116-117 *architectural project:* SAMA ARQUITECTOS, rafael sama

118-119 *architectural project:* ABAX, fernando de haro, jesús fernández, omar fuentes y bertha figueroa

120 a 123 *architectural project:* G+A, ESTUDIO DE DISEÑO Y ARQUITECTURA, alejandro garzón abreu y alberto torres hurtado, *interior design:* teresa rivera de cuaik, *contributor:* eugenio muñoz calderón

124 a 127 *architectural and interior design project:* PASCAL ARQUITECTOS, carlos pascal y gerard pascal

128 a 131 *architectural and interior design project:* departamento de arquitectura adolfo domínguez & GRUPO CERO, *contributor:* GRUPO CERO, alonso rodríguez molleda

132 a 135 *architectural and interior design project:* félix blanco martínez, maría eugenia nava y guillermo martínez

136-137 *architectural project:* GRUPO ARQUITECH, juan josé sánchez-aedo, *contributor:* alejandro viniegra, *construction:* GRUPO DANHOS, *lighting:* DEPRO iluminación, joaquín jamaica, LUZ + FORMA y luis lozoya

138-139 (left and center) *architectural project:* GRUPO ARQUITECH, juan josé sánchez-aedo y alejandro elizondo, *contributors:* fernando ortega montoya y daniel camacho flores, *structural work:* aguilar ingenieros consultores, *sewage system:* garza maldonado y asociados, *electrical work:* ingeniería A.G., *air conditioning:* IACSA, *lighting:* DEPRO iluminación, *closed circuit work:* GT-DF, (right) *architectural project:* GRUPO ARQUITECH, juan josé sánchez-aedo y alejandro elizondo, *contributor:* miguel ángel garcía

140-141 *architectural project:* GRUPO ARQUITECH, juan josé sánchez-aedo y alejandro elizondo, VIDARQ, abraham cherem cassab y david jasqui roffe, *contributor:* francisco materola y gabriel tabachnik, *lighting:* L+F, *construction:* VIDARQ, jacobo cherem ades y jaime agami

142 a 144 *architectural project:* CINEMEX, *interior design:* ART ARQUITECTOS, antonio rueda ventosa

145 a 147 *architectural and interior design project:* ART ARQUITECTOS, antonio rueda ventosa y sergio gutiérrez

149 *architectural project:* GLR ARQUITECTOS, gilberto I. rodríguez, *contributors:* bernardo chapa, caty fernández y tomas güereña

150-151 *architectural project:* DPGa, daniel pérez-gil, *project design contributor:* sergio reinoso ochoa, *project development contributors:* armando martínez montes y juan alberto fragoso, *furniture and fittings:* ezequiel farca y moda in casa

152 a 155 *architectural project:* D+S ARQUITECTOS, allan dayan askenazi y sonny sutton askenazi, *contributors:* alberto pérez fuentes, misael núñez lópez, ricardo gonzález gasca y susana díaz velasco

156 a 159 *architectural and interior design project:* PABLO MARTÍNEZ LANZ ARQUITECTOS, *contributors:* thenar ramón roura, joaquín pineda, josé luis trujano y jesús jauregui

160-161 *architectural project:* BUNKER ARQUITECTURA, jorge arteaga, esteban suárez, sebastián suárez y santiago becerra, *contributors:* paola moire, miguel ángel martínez, diana arroyo y jimena muhlia

162 a 165 *construction:* JUAN CARLOS AVILÉS ARQUITECTOS, *architectural project:* JUAN CARLOS AVILÉS ARQUITECTOS, juan carlos aviles iguiniz y sergio ruiz. *contributors:* juan carlos aviles iguiniz, sergio ruiz y rodrigo capistrán sánchez

166-167 *architectural project:* ABAX, fernando de haro, jesús fernández, omar fuentes y bertha figueroa

168-169 *architectural project:* ART ARQUITECTOS, antonio rueda ventosa, *interior design:* BERRY DESIGN GROUP, cassandra berry y antonio rueda ventosa

170-171 *architectural project:* ADIDAS GLOBAL, *proyect executions:* GRUPO CERO, alonso rodríguez molleda

172 173 *architectural project:* SPACE, juan carlos baumgartner y loreto rodríguez, *contributors:* luis monroy y jorge armendáriz, *lighting design:* LUA, *general contract work:* GAYA

174 *architectural and interior design project:* ART ARQUITECTOS, antonio rueda ventosa

175 (top) *architectural and interior design project:* ART ARQUITECTOS, antonio rueda ventosa, (bottom) *architectural project:* AGRAZ ARQUITECTOS, ricardo agraz

176-177 *architectural project:* GRUPO LBC, alfonso lópez baz, javier calleja y gonzalo martínez, *contributors:* simón hamui

178-179 *architectural project:* oscar m. cadona, *contributors:* sandra fernández, israel gómez, daniela navarrete y aranzazú fernández, *engineering:* alberto prieto, javier martínez y arturo morelos, *construction:* isidoro méndez

180-181 *architectural project:* ABAX, fernando de haro, jesús fernández, omar fuentes y bertha figueroa

182 183 *architectural project:* DPGA, daniel pérez-gil, *contributors:* sergio reinoso, ricardo zepeda, armando martínez, jorge vázquez, humberto rodríguez y pablo rodríguez

184 185 *architectural and interior design project:* FORMA ARQUITECTOS, eduardo ávalos, miguel de llano y josé segués

186 187 *architectural project:* SPACE, juan carlos baumgartner, *contributors:* adolfo arévalo y carlos juárez

188 *architectural project:* TARME, alex carranza valles y gerardo ruiz díaz, *furniture and fittings:* MARQCO, mariangel álvarez y covadonga hernández, *lighting:* MANTENIMIENTO ARQUITECTÓNICO INTEGRAL, pedro garza, *image design:* IASTY CONCEPTS, roberto sublayrolles, *contributors:* david baez tenorio, miguel darío, josé antonio saldaña, marco antonio garcía, alfredo arenas e israel garcía

190 a 193 *architectural project:* GRUPO CERO y ROCKWELL GROUP, *construction:* GRUPO CERO

194 a 197 *architectural and interior design project:* PASCAL ARQUITECTOS, carlos pascal y gerard pascal

198 a 201 *architectural project:* SAMA ARQUITECTOS, rafael sama

202-203 *architectural project:* ARQUITECH, juan josé sánchez-aedo, *contributors:* andrés santos

204 a 207 *architectural and interior design project:* félix blanco martínez, maría eugenia nava y guillermo martínez

208-209 *architectural project:* ADIDAS GLOBAL, *proyect executions:* GRUPO CERO, alonso rodríguez molleda

210-211 *architectural and interior design project:* ABAX, fernando de haro, jesús fernández, omar fuentes y bertha figueroa

212 a 215 *concept:* javier sordo madaleno, *concept development:* josé ma. zarazúa y jorge isaías guerrero, *architectural project:* javier sordo madaleno y jorge isaías guerrero, *construction:* DECOSA

216-217 *architectural project:* MARTOR ARQUITECTOS, enrique martorell y juan ricardo torres-landa, *contributors:* alejandro de noriega y mariana rodríguez

218-219 *architectural project:* ARQUITECH, juan josé sánchez-aedo y alejandro elizondo, *contributor:* aáron mendoza, *lighting:* DEPRO ILUMINACIÓN, joaquín jamaica

221 *architectural project:* JSª, javier sánchez, juan carral, julián martínez, julia cerruti, leticia nuñez y angélica soberanes

222-223 *architectural project:* BECKER ARQUITECTOS, moisés becker, *structural design:* aguilar ingenieros consultores s.c., *contributors:* salomón ison, eugenio romero, benjamín villeda y faustino reyes

224 (top left and bottom right) *architectural project:* JSª, javier sánchez, juan carral, julián martínez, julia cerruti, leticia nuñez y angélica soberanes, (top right) *architectural project and construction:* HASBANI ARQUITECTOS, mayer hasbani, *diseño estructural:* CTC ingenieros civiles, *consultancy:* manuel larrosa irigoyen, *contributors:* verónica elizalde, omar salas, paola arce, edgar r. reyes y enrique díaz lugo, *soil mechanics:* gutiérrez cimentaciones, *electrical, water supply and sanitary instalation:* MORI instalaciones, *air extraction:* DIMSA, (bottom left) *architectural project:* D+S ARQUITECTOS, allan dayan askenazi y sonny sutton askenazi, *contributors:* alberto pérez fuentes, misael núñez lópez, ricardo gonzález gasca y susana días velasco

225 (top left and bottom) *architectural project:* JSª, javier sánchez, juan carral, julián martínez, julia cerruti, leticia nuñez y angélica soberanes, (top right) *architectural project and construction:* HASBANI ARQUITECTOS, mayer hasbani, *structural design:* PESAMEX proyecto estructural s.a., *consultancy:* manuel larrosa irigoyen, *contributors:* verónica elizalde, omar salas y josé luis rodríguez

226 a 229 *architectural project:* GFA, GF+G y HOK, *interior design:* GFA + HOK, *furniture design:* ezequiel farca, *contributors:* josé askenazi, mónica garcía, liliana ramírez, carlos retiz y abraham farca.

230-231 *architectural project and construction:* HASBANI ARQUITECTOS, mayer hasbani, *structural design:* PESAMEX proyecto estructural s.a., *consultancy:* manuel larrosa irigoyen, *contributors:* verónica elizalde, omar salas y josé luis rodríguez

232 a 235 *architectural project:* MIGDAL ARQUITECTOS, jaime varon, abraham metta y alex metta

236 a 241 *architectural project:* JSª, javier sánchez, jorge ambrosi, carlos malagnon, juan carral, mario nájera, julián barnabe, giovanni f. oteiza y patricia aceves

242 a 245 *architectural and interior design project:* ABAX, fernando de haro, jesús fernández, omar fuentes y bertha figueroa, *contributor:* javier espinosa

246 a 249 *executive and interior design project:* guillermo almazán, gerardo varela y juan antonio encinas, *contributors:* dirk thurmer franssen, benjamín gastón muñoz, sandra ortiz bethencourt e isabel madera

250-251 *architectural and interior design project:* pedro escobar f.v., jorge escalante p., jorge carral d. y maría c. escamilla r., *contributors:* claudia tamayo castro, irma graciela gil sánchez, fernando hernández juárez, jesús torres carreño y oscar malpica cruz

252-253 *architectural project:* JSª, javier sánchez, paola calzada, larissa kadner y alejandro zárate

254 a 257 *architectural and museographic design:* MUSEOTEC, *architecture:* francisco lópez-guerra almada, antonio toca f., ramón alonso, edgar león, josé pablo ballesteros y francisco lópez guerra l., *museography:* georgina larrea, georgina lópez-guerra l. y ramón burillo, *coordination:* francisco ornelas, carlos camacho y marco aurelio torres h., *construction and customization:* TANSHEISHA CO. LTD, gavira producciones

photographic fotográficos photographiques fotografische

adrián montes - pgs. 71(bottom), 74-75, 216-217.

alberto moreno - pgs. 145 a 147.

alejandro rodríguez - pg. (bottom)149.

alfonso de béjar - pgs. 120 a 123, 210-211.

allen vallejo - pgs. 46-47, 244-245.

antonio pavón - pgs. 98 a 101.

bevin bering - pgs. 168-169

claude vogel - pgs. 166-167.

daniel galindo sánchez - pgs. 152 a 155, 224
(bottom left).

federico de jesús - pgs. 62-63, 184-185.

fernando cordero - pgs. 156-157, 158(top), 159, 212 a
215, 222-223.

héctor armando herrera - pgs. 14-15, 24-25, 66 a 69,
82-83, 112-115, 128 a 131, 150-151, 170-171, 182-183, 190
a 193, 208-209.

héctor velasco facio - pgs. 4-5, 9, 10(left), 20 a 23, 42, 44-45,
50-51, 76-77, 88-89, 90-91, 94-95, 102-103, 118-119, 162 a
165, 178 a 181, 188, 242-243.

jacob sadrak - pgs. 186-187.

jaime navarro - pgs. 10(right), 70, 71(top and center),
72-73, 78 a 81, 84 a 87, 124 a 127, 194 a 197, 252-253.

jordi farré - pgs. 64-65, 142 a 144, 250-251.

jorge del olmo - pgs. 176-177.

jorge rodríguez almanza - pgs. 11(left), 26-27, 90(right),
116-117, 198 a 201.

jorge silva - pgs. 254 a 257.

jorge taboada - pg. (top)149.

josé gallardo - pgs. 56-57.

juan josé diaz infante - pgs. 106-107.

leonardo walter - pgs. 18-19.

luis gordoa - pgs. 3, 48-49, 52, 53(top), 54-55, 90(center),
108, 110-111, 132 a 135, 138 a 141, 202 a 204, 206-207,
218-219, 221, 224(top left and bottom right), 225 (top
left and bottom left), 236 a 241.

marisol paredes - pgs. 36-37, 60-61, 174, 175(top).

megs inniss - pgs. 160-161.

mito covarrubias - pgs. 30-31, 175(bottom).

paul czitrom - pgs. 8, 11(right), 28-29, 58-59, 92, 136-137,
226 a 229, 232-235, 246-249.

santiago barreiro - pgs. 16-17, 32 a 35, 38 a 41, 96-97,
104-105, 172-173, 186-187.

sófocles hernández - pg. 158(bottom).

víctor jiménez - pgs. 224(top right), 225(top right),
230-231.

undine pröhl - pg. 53(center and bottom)

Se terminó de imprimir el mes de Enero del 2010 en China. El cuidado de la edición estuvo a cargo de AM Editores S.A. de C.V. Printed in January 2010 in China. Published by AM Editores S.A. de C.V.